Roadmap
to the
Heart of God

- - - - - - - - - - - - - - - - -

Nancy J McLoughlin

WESTBOW
P R E S S
A DIVISION OF THOMAS NELSON

Scripture quotations taken from the Holy Bible, New Living Translation, copyright 1996, 2004. Used by permission of Tyndale House Publishers, Inc., Wheaton, Illinois 60189. All rights reserved.

Scripture taken from the Holy Bible, New International Version®. Copyright © 1973, 1978, 1984 Biblica. Used by permission of Zondervan. All rights reserved.

WestBow Press books may be ordered through booksellers or by contacting:

WestBow Press
A Division of Thomas Nelson
1663 Liberty Drive
Bloomington, IN 47403
www.westbowpress.com
1-(866) 928-1240

Because of the dynamic nature of the Internet, any web addresses or links contained in this book may have changed since publication and may no longer be valid. The views expressed in this work are solely those of the author and do not necessarily reflect the views of the publisher, and the publisher hereby disclaims any responsibility for them.

Any people depicted in stock imagery provided by Thinkstock are models, and such images are being used for illustrative purposes only.

Certain stock imagery © Thinkstock.

ISBN: 978-1-4497-4474-8 (sc)
ISBN: 978-1-4497-4473-1 (e)

Library of Congress Control Number: 2012905453

Printed in the United States of America

WestBow Press rev. date: 04/26/2012

TABLE OF CONTENTS

TOPICAL INDEX

Prologue

Most Christians long in the deep recesses of their souls to have a close, intimate relationship with their Heavenly Father, but eventually find out that actually achieving this goal seems next to impossible. Either they think they've already reached the peak of heavenly, relational intimacy even though it doesn't really bring the satisfaction they anticipated, or they give up and quit in despair.

The good news is that there's a roadmap showing us the way to the heart of God, and it's clearly laid out in Scripture if we search for it. God has designed this joy-filled, soul-satisfying, contentment-producing relationship with Him in such a way that it only comes about if we really want it with all our hearts and are willing to pursue it relentlessly. (*"Then you will call upon me and come and pray to me, and I will listen to you. You will seek me and find me when you seek me with all your heart."* Jeremiah 29:12-13 NIV).

Unfortunately, the world around us and our own selfish, lazy natures conspire to keep us looking for the easy way, the simple way, the comfortable way, and yes, the logical way to find a God who is only accessed through spirit-to-spirit communication. Only as we're willing to humble ourselves under His mighty hand, trust Him completely, and obey Him instantly no matter how hard that action might be, will we find this incredible friendship that we were created to enjoy.

The following twenty-three chapters, when taken with a big gulp of humility and swallowed with a huge dose of courage, will lead you on a wild, exciting adventure of coming to know the heart of the God of the Universe. Each chapter covers a stand-alone topic that, when assimilated into your thought process, will lead you a step closer to finding that incredible place where you know and embrace the truth that you're a treasured child of the Most High God. As you walk through each subject, reading it with an open heart, dissecting it through answering the questions, and seeking the wisdom of the Holy Spirit to put your new knowledge into practice, you will find yourself traveling on a collision course with an intense, perfect love. At last you will come into complete union with your "Wonderful Counselor, Mighty God, Everlasting Father, Prince of Peace" (Isaiah 9:6), the One your heart has longed for since time began.

So, fasten up your seatbelts and join me for the ride of your life—the one that will open your eyes, turn your world upside down, scare you half to death, and bring you the best life God has to offer you!

Chapter 1

HELP! I'VE FALLEN AND I CAN'T GET UP!

Oh, no! The unthinkable has happened! My worst fears have come true, and the resulting wound to my heart is horrific. I'm in shock and can hardly believe this is happening to me. "What did I do to deserve this wound?" I wonder. "Am I such an awful person that I have to be punished this way? Is this pain my fault somehow?" I shout my grief into the empty darkness over and over, but all I hear is an echo of my anguish. Because of the shock and disbelief I'm experiencing, I keep forgetting what happened until I'm jerked back into the reality of my wound. Each time I crawl into denial, I am constantly snatched back to face the truth. It's like being stabbed with a knife all over again, cutting my wound deeper and wider until it becomes a jagged mess. "Will I ever live through this pain?" I question others and God. "Will I ever stop crying? Will I ever have joy again or think life is worth living?"

As I begin to sink beneath the surface of my heartache, I wonder if **anyone** makes it through life without being wounded, and yet as I look around me, most people look happy. How can that be? Are they just pretending? I know I'm tempted to pretend because I don't want people to see me in this vulnerable, weak state of mind, unable to pull myself together day after day. I feel so lost, so hopeless, without direction or focus on anything other than my pain. I can't seem to hear God's voice speaking to me, and to tell the truth, I'm kind of disappointed and hurt that He would let me go through this pain in the first place. I don't want anyone to know the depth of my wound, or to judge me (what if they think I'm to blame for it?!), or criticize the way I'm handling it. As

I continue to compare my brokenness with other people's happiness under the same set of circumstances, I come to the conclusion, "If most people ARE wounded, there has be a way to continue walking while wounded, and these people have found the secret."

I turn my attention to wondering what the solution is. The first thought that comes to my mind is whether or not the answer involves pretending. Is it okay to pretend? Do I have to wear my wound like a badge? I see some people pour out their woes on anyone that will listen, and I don't want to be that kind of person! On the other hand, I see people who never process their pain and become bitter, angry people, and I don't want to turn out that way either. I turn to God's word and, of course, it has the answer. Psalm 34:18 says, *"The LORD is close to the brokenhearted; he rescues those whose spirits are crushed."* Now I understand that the healing only comes from the Lord, and that it is HIS job to bind up the brokenhearted. Does that mean, though, that I should just hide my wound and not share it with anyone while the Lord is in the process of healing? Well, it appears that other people are also part of the healing process. Here's what Paul says in 1 Thessalonians 5:14, *"Brothers and sisters, we urge you to warn those who are lazy. Encourage those who are timid. Take tender care of those who are weak. Be patient with everyone.* Perhaps the idea is that we only share our hurts with those who are safe like a trusted friend, a Christian counselor, a compassionate pastor, or a fellow sufferer. After all, it does say in 2 Corinthians 1:4, *"He comforts us in all our troubles so that we can comfort others. When they are troubled, we will be able to give them the same comfort God has given us."* Who better to bare our wounds to than someone who's been there and survived!

What if I CHOOSE to hide my wound just because it's so painful and I don't want to have to relive it, let alone cry or look weak; you know, the suffer-in-secret kind of behavior. Is that okay? Well, according to my counselor friends, there's value and healing in actually walking back through the hurtful situation while learning appropriate coping skills. What if it's also important to OWN our woundedness so we can gain a healthier perspective allowing us to get up and continue walking? After all God does promise that these troubles will continue to happen throughout life. (1 Peter 4:12, *"Dear friends, do not be surprised at the painful trial you are suffering, as though something strange were happening to you.*"). Maybe that's why God has something to say about acknowledging our mistakes out loud because they often contribute to the pain in our lives. Maybe that's how we find these secrets to walking while wounded. He says, "*Confess your sins to each other and pray for each other so that you may be healed. The earnest prayer of a righteous person has great power and produces wonderful results.*" (James 5:16).

"Well," I think to myself, "I'll just hurry and get this sharing time over with so I can get on with my life. I'm tired of being sad and discouraged. I want to get back to being strong and confident instead of weak and filled with disgust for who I've become." A new thought hits me! What if God's greatest desire for me **isn't** to be strong and in control? What if this brokenness is God's perfect opportunity to work in my life and teach me to be humble? He does say in 2 Corinthians 12:9-10, "*But he said to me, "My grace is sufficient for you, for my power is made perfect in weakness." Therefore I will boast all the more gladly about my weaknesses, so that Christ's power may rest on me. That is why, for Christ's sake, I delight in weaknesses, in insults, in hardships, in persecutions, in difficulties. For when I am weak, then I am strong.*" Can I handle being weak and fragile? Can I believe that this woundedness I carry around like a heavy burden will actually become my greatest asset from God's perspective? Am I willing to allow my pain to be used by the Lord to help other freshly damaged comrades find hope, so they, too, will learn to walk while wounded? "Who knows," I say as I fling out my hand in surrender to the Lord's will for my pain, "God may take my ugly, oozing wound and turn it into an eye-catching, attractive BEAUTY MARK!"

----

1. Have you ever sustained one of these life-shattering kinds of wounds? If so, what was it and how long ago did it take place? _____

_____

_____

_____

2. What are your honest feelings toward this wound? Is the wound in your head (a cultural wound, a denominational wound, an up-bringing wound, a misunderstanding, or a miscommunication), or in your heart (an offense to your personhood, an offense to your worth, or an offense to your intellect)? Have you run the question, "What is the truth?" past both the head and the heart wounds? If so, what was the result?

_____

_____

_____

_____

3. On a scale of 0-10, how much healing has taken place so far on your wound? Are you walking yet or are you still flat on your back? _____

_____

_____

_____

4. Who have you shared your wound with? How did that turn out?

_____

_____

_____

_____

5. Have you seen any sign yet of God turning this wound into good for you? If so, how? If not, how do you feel about that? _____

_____

_____

_____

6. How do you handle the weak, vulnerable part of being wounded?

_____

_____

_____

_____

7. What do you think of pretending and putting on a strong front after being wounded? On the other hand, have you ever felt as though you said too much about your wound? How did you handle those feelings?

_____

_____

_____

_____

8. How do you feel toward other wounded people in your life? Do you feel tender toward them? Or do you feel like you need to run away because their pain reminds you too much of your own pain?

_____

_____

_____

_____

9. Now that you've focused on being wounded, do you know or suspect that there are more deep wounds in your heart? If so, use the rest of this page to describe them, write down how you feel about them, and determine where you are in the healing process. Have you seen any good come out of them yet? If so, describe God's possible reasons for allowing you to be wounded in the first place. If not, how do you handle waiting for His goodness to show up? _____

_____

_____

_____

_____

_____

_____

_____

_____

_____

_____

_____

_____

_____

_____

_____

_____

_____

_____

_____

_____

_____

_____

_____

_____

_____

_____

_____

_____

_____

_____

_____

_____

_____

_____

Chapter 2

OKAY, SO I'VE BEEN WOUNDED— NOW WHAT?

All right, fine! I'm agreeing that I'm wounded. Now what do I do with all the pain and helplessness my admission costs me? At least pretending and staying in denial allows me to "kick the can down the road," and delay the grieving, writhing, teeth-gnashing process. Now that I'm choosing to live in reality, the constant, debilitating pain threatens to do me in at any moment. How do I stave off the feelings that disaster is just around the corner, or that I'm not going to survive this wound?

Once again I turn to God's Word, and once again, I'm surprised to find the answer! God actually questions me in His Word as though I should KNOW the answer, and maybe I do. Maybe I'm just too afraid to try His solutions. *"Have you never heard? Have you never understood? The Lord is the everlasting God, the Creator of all the earth. He never grows weak or weary. No one can measure the depths of his understanding. He gives power to the weak and strength to the powerless. Even youths will become weak and tired, and young men will fall in exhaustion. But those who trust in the Lord will find new strength. They will soar high on wings like eagles. They will run and not grow weary. They will walk and not faint."* Isaiah 4:28-31.

"I understand that this is the answer: '***But those who trust in the Lord will find new strength***.' I just don't know what that kind of trust LOOKS like," I say to the Lord. "I don't know how to trust when I don't FEEL any trust. Besides, You let me be wounded! How can I trust someone who doesn't take better care of me than THAT? By the way,

I have a few good ideas of my **own** on how to survive that I might want to try—is THAT so wrong? Also, how long will it take after I start trusting You before You send me the strength? I can't hang on much longer . . . ." As I think about what I just said to the Lord, I'm so glad God doesn't take offense at my questions, but prompts me to look further. Psalm 37:34 comes to my mind, *"Don't be impatient for the Lord to act! Keep traveling steadily along his pathway and in due season he will honor you with every blessing."* As I ponder God's words and wonder how I could ever quit being impatient, more verses come to me (Proverbs 3:5-6). Even though I know these verses by heart, I see them in a new light today. *"Trust in the Lord with all your heart,"* I recite. "I get it!" I say excitedly. The key to trusting is my choice to do it with ALL my heart, with everything in me, completely, no matter what logic shouts at me, with abandonment to HIS will instead of my own. *"Do not depend on your own understanding,"* I continue with my recitation. Well there you have it! God DOESN'T want me to try my own ideas. He doesn't want me to depend on my own thought processes at ALL, which is a hard pill for me to swallow. I move on to the next verse, *"Seek his will in all you do, and he will show you which path to take."* What? So now I have to seek HIS will in **everything** I do, and HE will show me what to do and how to survive? Wow! I don't think that if I wasn't so desperate, I would even consider doing what these verses command me to do. After all, they go against everything that seems right to me! "What's that you're saying, God? You know better than I do? Oh right, I remember that verse:"

"'My thoughts are nothing like your thoughts,' says the Lord. 'And my ways are far beyond anything you could imagine. For just as the heavens are higher than the earth, so my ways are higher than your ways and my thoughts higher than your thoughts.'" Isaiah 55:8-9. Well, I can't say I blame the Lord for giving me these kinds of directives. I haven't exactly done the best job possible with my life so far; I guess I have no other choice but to do things His way and actually have faith that He'll come through for me.

Now that I've made the choice to trust only the Lord and wait for His guidance, what do I do in the meantime? I'm still hurting and nothing has changed in my circumstances except to watch them to go from bad to worse! As I start to worry and fret, the thought comes to me to start putting into practice what I am choosing to do—and that's to ask the Lord for wisdom. Immediately, I remember a handout I received at a recent women's retreat and I race to find it. I can't believe the Lord is answering my prayer this quickly. Maybe trusting Him really does work! Once I find this handout, I realize it has the answers I'm searching for. The first section deals with basic survival skills—how I can make it through each day.

The Hang-On-To List When Enduring Panic, Pain, and Suffering

1. **Grab 2-3 verses and make them my mantra** (*"I can do all things through Christ who gives me strength."* Phil. 4:13, *"The LORD is close to the brokenhearted; He rescues those whose spirits are crushed."* Psalm 34:18, *"Don't be afraid, for I am with you. Don't be discouraged, for I am your God. I will strengthen you and help you. I will hold you up with my victorious right hand."* Isaiah 41:10, *"Don't worry about anything; instead, pray about everything. Tell God what you need, and thank him for all He has done."* Phil. 4:6, *"And we know that God causes everything to work together for the good of those who love God and are called according to His purpose for them."* Romans 8:28)

2. **Make an ongoing list of things to be thankful for and read it over and over** (big, little, and mundane, just so I can see the hand of the Lord in my life)

3. **Cry out to God with every thought I have** (He can handle my pain, fear, and frustration—I must take the temptation to indulge in "rabbit-trail" thinking and the "what if's", and turn them into prayer)

4. **Surround myself with supportive people** (restrict my time with those who aren't)

5. **Take good care of myself** (eat healthy, get exercise, get enough rest, and find things to celebrate—*"Don't be dejected and sad, for the joy of the Lord is your strength."* Nehemiah 8:10)

6. **Don't be hard on myself** (Crying isn't bad. God's children turn their backs on Him all the time so He understands my tears, and that's why He's close to the broken-hearted. Remember that just because I'm not appreciated by someone doesn't mean I'm not valuable. Also, I have to break up my day into manageable pieces and then celebrate when I make it through each section of my day instead of having unreasonable expectations)

7. **Don't get so caught up in my pain that I don't see the other wounded people out there** (I know they are all around me, and as I help others, some of my own pain is relieved)

I realize as I work through this list that all these suggestions actually do work if I choose to implement them. Once again, I'm faced with a choice to ask God for strength to do the right things if I want to survive this wound and find a way to keep walking in spite of it.

The next section of the handout gives warnings of the types of pitfalls that are common to hurting people:

The Temptations That Come From Being Wounded

1. Playing the blame game
2. Embracing false guilt
3. Having pity parties (It's not fair!)
4. Dumping on everyone—being "needy" in the hopes that someone will take care of me and make me feel better about myself
5. Withdrawing
6. Pretending to others that I'm doing better than I am
7. Trying to move on before I'm actually healed

8. Denying my woundedness to myself
9. Turning to food, distractions, substance abuse, shopping, etc. to ease the pain
10. Demanding that everyone around me be on my side
11. Having a hissy-fit—that behavior FEEDS the anger/pain monster rather than relieving it
12. Judging others when guilty of the same thing, to distract attention from myself

Ouch! I can see myself falling for every one of those temptations. It's a good thing I'm choosing to trust the Lord and not my own thought process and my own strength or I'd be in big trouble. Not only would I not have a hope of healing, my wound would result in me becoming very dysfunctional.

The final section of the handout contains only good news! Believe it or not, there are BLESSINGS that can actually come as a result of my wound.

The Blessings that come from being Wounded

1. Pain has a tendency to turn our focus to the Lord (2 Corinthians 7:9-10, *"Now I am glad I sent it (severe letter), not because it hurt you, but because the pain caused you to repent and change your ways. It was the kind of sorrow God wants his people to have . . . For the kind of sorrow God wants us to experience leads us away from sin and results in salvation."*)
2. Pain brings humility
3. Pain teaches us compassion for other hurting people
4. Pain gets rid of all the extraneous things in our lives
5. Pain forces us to gain wisdom
6. Pain gives us empathetic tools and credibility, and it opens doors of ministry to others

What wonderful joy I feel to think that all this pain I'm experiencing will result in good things coming into my life, and into the growth of my character! I can't believe the goodness of God who turns all this mess into gain for me. I think I can go on! I think I can wait patiently! I think I can see my way to even trusting the Lord with all my heart! After all, the alternative of trying to survive on my own isn't worth comparing to the things God has promised me if I let Him take over. Believe it or not, I think I'm feeling some excitement and hope cropping up in my spirit!

----

1. How does it feel to admit you're wounded? Explain _____
   _____
   _____
   _____

2. Has the pain gotten worse now that you're out of denial? If so, how do you feel about that new reality? _____
   _____
   _____
   _____

3. Does the idea of trusting only God excite you or scare you? Explain
   _____
   _____
   _____
   _____

4. Have you tried completely trusting God without any back-up plans from your own thought process? How did that turn out? Did you feel any strength coming from the Lord? Explain _____
   _____
   _____
   _____

5. What did you think of the survival cheat-sheet? Have you tried any of these suggestions? If so, how did they work? Give examples of what you've tried _____

_____

_____

_____

6. Were you surprised by the temptations that attack at the point of our greatest weakness? Have you fallen prey to any of them? If so, explain

_____

_____

_____

_____

7. Were you shocked to find out that your woundedness could actually produce blessings? Have you experienced any of these blessings yet? If so, give examples _____

_____

_____

_____

8. Do you think you can survive your wound and make a full recovery with these guidelines? Why or why not? Do you think you'll be better off for having been wounded? Why or why not? Can you see hope up ahead? Why or why not? _____

_____

_____

_____

Chapter 3

IS HOPE OVERRATED?

What if my life as I've always known it comes to an end? What if I've lost my last hope? What if all the support pillars I've counted on get knocked out from under me? What if my worst fears come true? What if I can't find a way up or out? Is there a formula out there that really works? Will God come through for me? For sure? Guaranteed?

As I asked these questions, I began to learn that God DOES have answers. He helped me understand that only HE could help me, but there was one caveat—I had to WANT His help (James 1:5-6, *"If any of you lacks wisdom, you should ask God, who gives generously to all without finding fault, and it will be given to you. But when you ask, you must believe and not doubt, because the one who doubts is like a wave of the sea, blown and tossed by the wind."*). Now that idea may sound strange—who wouldn't want help?—but I wanted easy, comfortable solutions, and I had a feeling His direction would be anything BUT easy. I began to think of my kids, though, and my eternity, my legacy, and my own desire for soul contentment. Did I care enough to make hard choices every minute of every day? Did I love my kids enough to change anything the Lord put His finger on, and to give up anything the Lord said had to go? What a dilemma! I almost gave up until I began playing out the scenario of NOT changing versus letting God have His way in my life. Finally, in desperation, I gave the Holy Spirit permission to have His way in my life!

The first thing He showed me was that I had to quit trying, striving, worrying, and fretting, which, not only was unproductive behavior, but those feelings and actions were keeping me from finding help. What a hard choice to make! Worrying and being anxious were as natural to me as breathing, and I wasn't sure I wanted to get out of my comfort zone. I know the Bible gives this promise, *"Then Jesus said, 'Come to me, all of you who are weary and carry heavy burdens, and I will give you rest. Take my yoke upon you. Let me teach you, because I am humble and gentle at heart, and you will find rest for your souls,'"* but what does that mean? I longed to rest, but how did I rest in the midst of such great pain and fear? Little by little, I found out that as I reached out to Him, and turned my agitated thoughts into prayers for help, He supernaturally poured peace and rest into my troubled heart.

Next, He prompted me to pray this prayer every day, **with all my heart**, asking continually for strength and wisdom to carry out His promptings. *"Search me, O God, and know my heart; test me and know my anxious thoughts. Point out anything in me that offends you, and lead me along the path of everlasting life."* Psalm 139:23-24. Of course, the way He used to search me was through His word, so I had to commit to finding a way to immerse myself in Scripture even when I didn't want to—even when it seemed dull and boring. Much to my surprise, though, I found that when I was obedient, He gave me a hunger for His word and showed me great treasure: words of comfort and strength when I was hurting so badly I was ready to give up, words of direction and wisdom that I didn't know existed, words of love that brought healing to my broken heart, and words of courage that helped me go on (*"So take a new grip with your tired hands and strengthen your weak knees. Mark out a straight path for your feet so that those who are weak and lame (*my own CHILDREN!*) will not fall but become strong."* Hebrews 12:12-13). He also used friends and the church to search me so I had to be willing to listen humbly and to faithfully attend church so I could hear His voice.

Finally the Lord brought all the verses to my attention that talk about giving thanks no matter what was happening in my life (*"Be thankful in all circumstances, for this is God's will for you who belong to Christ Jesus."* 1 Thessalonians 5:18). "How is that possible?" I wondered. "What if I don't FEEL thankful?" As I pondered such a strange command, I remembered the verses in Proverbs 3:5-6, *"Trust in the Lord with all your heart; do not depend on your own understanding. Seek his will in all you do, and he will show you which path to take."* Since He told me to trust Him, and since I so desperately needed and wanted help, I decided to obey. What happened next is truly amazing! The more I thanked Him, the more I found to thank Him for, and my heart became flooded with joy. Yes, you heard me right—I had joy in the midst of deep pain and heartache. Who knew that joy would ever come to me again?

As hard as it's been, and as much as I've wanted to quit at times, God's formula DOES work. The best part is that He gives strength and wisdom to follow it every single day—after all, He's far more committed to seeing His perfect masterpiece come to light (that would be ME!) than I ever could be. He's also longing to give me the chance to be part of His exciting kingdom work, and the opportunity to receive rewards and blessings in my future. What a sweet deal!

---

1. Have you ever felt like your last support was pulled out from under you? If so, how did that feel? Explain what happened _____

_____

_____

2. Have you ever asked God for wisdom? Why or why not? If so, what happened? _____

_____

_____

3. What or who is important enough to you to make you willing to follow only God's leading and to change or give up anything He asks you to? Why did you answer as you did? _____

_____

_____

4. Has God ever asked you to do anything that you've refused to do? If so, why did you refuse? _____

_____

_____

_____

5. On a scale of 0-10, how much of each day do you spend in some form of worrying or fretting? What do you mostly worry about? Why?

_____

_____

_____

_____

6. What percentage of your worrying time are you able to turn into prayer? Explain _____

_____

_____

_____

7. Have you ever prayed the "Search me, Oh God" prayer? Why or why not? If so, what was the outcome? _____

_____

_____

_____

8. How good are you at remembering to be thankful in all circumstances? When you do remember, how does it affect your attitude? What helps you remember to be thankful? _____

_____

_____

_____

Chapter 4

MY FEAR FACTOR IS OFF THE CHARTS!

"Oh, no, please, God, don't ask me to say anything to them, or do something that might direct negative attention my way. I'm way too afraid to attempt to be forthright or honest or assertive. I don't like feeling uncomfortable and worrying that people won't like me. Please just let me ignore the problem. Besides, it's not my business anyway, right? What are you saying, Lord? It IS my business if you ask me to intervene? But if you wanted me to be that kind of brave, courageous person, why did you make me so fearful? You DIDN'T? You told me that in your Word??" Quickly, I raced for my Bible, and sure enough, there it was right in plain sight! 2 Timothy 1:7 says very clearly, "*For God has not given us a spirit of fear and timidity, but of power, love, and self-discipline.*"

"Well, Lord," I complained. "If it isn't you making me so fearful, who or what is causing all this agitation?" I heard nothing more as I pondered my intense desire to "stay out of the line of fire." I knew that fear was holding me back from completely obeying the Lord, and the more I thought about my level of fear, the more intrigued I became over its origin. I pulled out my collegiate dictionary and turned to the word "fear". I was shocked at how my nemesis was described: **A distressing emotion aroused by impending danger, evil, pain, etc., whether the threat is real or imagined; concern or anxiety."**

"How crazy is that?" I thought to myself. "I have the same emotion whether the danger is real or imagined! What if I'm choosing to be fearful when there's no reason to have that distressing emotion? What if I'm reacting poorly, making bad choices, and becoming emotionally paralyzed for NOTHING?" My thesaurus was right next to my dictionary so I looked up synonyms for fear hoping to shed more light on my deep addiction, and the intensity of the words used surprised me as much as the definition did: **Apprehension, consternation, dismay, terror, fright, panic, horror, trepidation, anxiety, cowardice, worry, insecurity, timidity, need to control, fretting and agitation."**

"Okay, Lord," I remonstrated. "I'm not THAT bad! I just want to 'fly under the radar.' I believe in 'live and let live.' What's wrong with taking the easy, safe way out in every situation? After all, who says I'm even right in what I'm thinking or feeling about a particular situation? What if I stick my neck out and go through all that turmoil only to find out I'm wrong? Besides, I have high blood pressure and my doctor told me to avoid unnecessary stress! You need to find someone else to do the confronting business, especially since I think most issues will eventually work themselves out if left alone and given enough time. What did you say, Lord? The problems **don't** just go away? Well, even if that's true, You must not know me very well. I CAN'T just quit being apprehensive. It's impossible!" Satisfied that I had finally convinced the Lord of my unsuitability to do what He was asking of me, I went to sit at my computer and check my e-mails. The thought crossed my mind to put the word "fear" into Google and see what came up. Once again I was amazed at what I discovered. My research showed me that fear can manifest itself in more than one way. As I summarized all the information in front of me, I realized that sometimes fear shows itself as a startled, panic feeling based on outside influences. Other times, though, it shows itself as a gut-wrenching, hand-wringing anxiety that leads people to worry and even obsess over what might happen. Anxiety tends to hang on, paralyzing people's minds and propelling them into controlling behaviors of all sorts. Worry, obsessing, and controlling go hand-in-hand and they stem from fear. "That's ME!" I blurted. "I feel exactly like that, and I do all those kinds of things. I feel trapped and helpless and so full of anxiety all the time because of my fear! Why am I that way?" I wondered. "What's beneath the surface that makes me react out of this deep-seated distrust of what's going to happen next?" I continued my research and found that all these fears have been thoroughly researched and categorized into four areas:

1. Fear of existence (how and when will I die? Will something bad happen to me?)
2. Fear of abandonment (Will I be left alone?)
3. Fear of negative self-esteem (How will people view me? Will they dislike me? Will they think I'm a failure?)
4. Fear of fear itself (Phobophobia—the phenomenon of severe fears and anxieties)

I sat in absolute astonishment as I began to understand that two out of the four categories described my fears perfectly! I realized that these fears are not genetic in origin—they are learned behavior from either watching my role models act out of their own fears or because of negative events I've experienced. The sad thing is that my fear never fixes anything; rather it paralyzes me, rendering me unable to find a solution for my problems. It keeps my mind, thoughts, and emotions in turmoil, and keeps me unable to hear the voice of the Lord or seek His council. No wonder God made it so clear that He didn't give me a spirit of fear! He has to hate what fear is doing to His beloved child—rendering me incapable of becoming the best version of myself.

I reached for my Bible again and found out that it's full of verses reminding us not to be fearful. Evidently I must not be the only weak-kneed, lily-livered, yellow-bellied, chicken-hearted child He has! The verses admonishing me to reject my constant sense of foreboding just went on and on: Joshua 1:9, *"This is my command—be strong and courageous! Do not be afraid or discouraged. For the Lord your God is with you wherever you go."* Psalms 34:4, *"I prayed to the Lord, and He answered me. He freed me from all my fears."* Psalm 46:1-3, *"God is our refuge and strength, always ready to help in times of trouble. So we will not fear when earthquakes come and the mountains crumble into the sea. Let the oceans roar and foam. Let the mountains tremble as the waters surge!"* Psalm 27:1-3, *"The Lord is my light and my salvation—so why should I be afraid? The Lord is my fortress, protecting me from danger, so why should I tremble? When evil people come to devour me, when my enemies and foes attack me, they will stumble and fall. Though a mighty army surrounds me, my heart will not be afraid. Even if I am attacked, I will remain confident."* Psalms 91:1-7,

11-12, 14-16, "*Those who live in the shelter of the Most High will find rest in the shadow of the Almighty. This I declare about the Lord: He alone is my refuge, my place of safety; he is my God, and I trust him. For he will rescue you from every trap and protect you from deadly disease. He will cover you with his feathers. He will shelter you with his wings. His faithful promises are your armor and protection. Do not be afraid of the terrors of the night, nor the arrow that flies in the day. Do not dread the disease that stalks in darkness, nor the disaster that strikes at midday. Though a thousand fall at your side, though ten thousand are dying around you, these evils will not touch you. For he will order his angels to protect you wherever you go. They will hold you up with their hands so you won't even hurt your foot on a stone. The Lord says, "I will rescue those who love me. I will protect those who trust in my name. When they call on me, I will answer; I will be with them in trouble. I will rescue and honor them. I will reward them with a long life and give them my salvation.*" Matthew 10:29-31, "*But not a single sparrow can fall to the ground without your Father knowing it. And the very hairs on your head are all numbered. So don't be afraid; you are more valuable to God than a whole flock of sparrows.*" Philippians 4:6-7, "*Don't worry about anything; instead, pray about everything. Tell God what you need, and thank Him for all He has done. Then you will experience God's peace which exceeds anything we can understand. His peace will guard your hearts and minds as you live in Christ Jesus.*"

As I read through these verses, I saw a theme emerging. Not only does God never react to His children's fear with anger, disgust, or frustration, He tells us in each verse WHY we don't have to be afraid. I realized that He understands how prone to fear we are, and He's doing everything in His power to help us overcome this terrible obstacle to becoming all He has in mind for us. I began to understand that He actually gives us ANTIDOTES for our fear. He starts out by showing us where our fear originates. **Fear actually comes from not believing that God really loves us with a perfect love**. (1 John 4:18, "*Such love has no fear, because perfect love expels all fear. If we are afraid, it is for fear of punishment, and this shows that we have not fully experienced His perfect love.*") Now that I knew where my fear came from, I went on to discover all these antidotes as I looked at each verse:

1. **Remembering to pray about our fears** (Philippians 4:6, "*Don't worry about anything; instead, pray about everything. Tell God what you need, and thank Him for all He has done.*")

2. **Believing God will always be there for us (Isaiah 41:10, "***Don't be afraid, for I am with you. Don't be discouraged, for I am your God. I will strengthen you and help you. I will hold you up with my victorious right hand.*")

3. **Knowing God is our protector (Psalm 27:1-2, "***The Lord is my light and my salvation—so why should I be afraid? The Lord is my fortress, protecting me from danger, so why should I tremble? When evil people come to devour me, when my enemies and foes attack me, they will stumble and fall.*")

4. **Focusing our minds on Jesus (Hebrews 12:1b-2a, "***And let us run with endurance the race God has set before us. We do this by keeping our eyes on Jesus, the champion who initiates and perfects our faith.*")

5. **Finding refuge and strength in God (Psalms 62:7-8, "***My victory and honor come from God alone. He is my refuge, a rock where no enemy can reach me. O my people, trust in Him at all times. Pour out your heart to Him, for God is our refuge.*")

6. **Praising God (1 Thessalonians 5:18, "***Be thankful in all circumstances, for this is God's will for you who belong to Christ Jesus.*")

7. **Knowing God is holding us steady (Isaiah 43:1-2, " . . . Do** *not be afraid, for I have ransomed you. I have called you by name; you are mine. When you go through deep waters, I will be with you. When you go through rivers of difficulty, you will not drown. When you walk through the fire of oppression, you will not be burned up; the flames will not consume you.*")

8. **Remembering that God has promised to always be with us (Matthew 28:20,** "*And be sure of this: I am with you always, even to the end of the age.*")

9. **Understanding our incredible value and worth to God (Romans 8:15-17,** "*So you have not received a spirit that makes you fearful slaves. Instead, you received God's Spirit when He adopted you as His own children. Now we call Him, 'Abba, Father.' For His Spirit joins with our spirit to affirm that we are God's children. And since we are His children, we are His heirs. In fact, together with Christ we are heirs of God's glory.*")

10. **Comprehending God's individualized approach to us (Psalms 139:1-18** " . . . *You made all the delicate, inner parts of my body and knit me together in my mother's womb. Thank you for making me so wonderfully complex! Your workmanship is marvelous—how well I know it. You watched me as I was being formed in utter seclusion, as I was woven together in the dark of the womb. You saw me before I was born. Every day of my life was recorded in your book. Every moment was laid out before a single day had passed* . . . ."*)

11. **Exercising faith in God's promises (Psalms 56: 3-4, 9-11,** "*But when I am afraid, I will put my trust in you. I praise God for what He has promised. I trust in God, so why should I be afraid? What can mere mortals do to me? My enemies will retreat when I call to you for help. This I know: God is on my side! I praise God for what He has promised; Yes, I praise the Lord for what He has promised. I trust in God, so why should I be afraid? What can mere mortals do to me?*")

12. **Knowing God will comfort us in our struggles (2 Corinthians 1:3-5,** "*All praise to God, the Father of our Lord Jesus Christ. God is our merciful Father and the source of all comfort. He comforts us in all our troubles so that we can comfort others. When they are troubled, we will be able to give them the same comfort He has given us. For the more we suffer for Christ, the more God will shower us with His comfort through Christ.*")

13. **Feeling God's peace which He promises to give us (Philippians 4:7,** "*Then you will experience God's peace, which exceeds anything we can understand. His peace will guard your hearts and minds as you live in Christ Jesus.*")

14. **Understanding that fear does not come from God (2 Timothy 1:7,** "*For God has not given us a spirit of fear and timidity, but of power, love, and self-discipline.*")

15. **Knowing God will keep us safe (Psalms 118:5-7,** "*In my distress I prayed to the Lord, and the Lord answered me and set me free. The Lord is for me, so I will have no fear. What can mere people do to me? Yes, the Lord is for me; He will help me. I will look in triumph at those who hate me.*")

16. **Understanding that He is our rescuer (Hebrews 13:5-6,** "*Don't love money; be satisfied with what you have. For God has said, 'I will never fail you. I will never abandon you.' So we can say with confidence, 'The Lord is my helper, so I will have no fear. What can mere people do to me?'*")

17. **Seeing that worry and fear can't fix our problems; in fact, they make them worse (Matthew 6:25-34,** "*Therefore I tell you, do not worry about your life, what you will eat or drink; or about your body, what you will wear. Is not life more than food, and the body more than clothes? Look at the birds of the air; they do not sow or reap or store away in barns, and yet your heavenly Father feeds them. Are you not much more valuable than they? Can any one of you by worrying add a single hour to your life? And why do you worry about clothes? See how the flowers of the field grow. They do not labor or spin. Yet I tell you that not even Solomon in all his splendor was dressed like one of these. If that is how God clothes the grass of the field, which is here today and tomorrow is thrown into the fire, will he not much more clothe you—you of little faith? So do not worry, saying, 'What shall we eat?' or 'What shall we drink?' or 'What shall we wear?' For the pagans*

run after all these things, and your heavenly Father knows that you need them. But seek first his kingdom and his righteousness, and all these things will be given to you as well. Therefore do not worry about tomorrow, for tomorrow will worry about itself. Each day has enough trouble of its own.")

18. **Having confidence in God's faithfulness (Mark 4:40, "Then He asked them,** '*Why are you afraid? Do you still have no faith?'"*)

19. **Recognizing that He sends His angels to watch over us (Psalm 91:11-12, "***For He will order His angels to protect you wherever you go. They will hold you up with their hands so you won't even hurt your foot on a stone."*)

20. **Remembering that God is trustworthy (Proverbs 3:5-6, "***Trust in the Lord with all your heart; do not depend on your own understanding. Seek his will in all you do, and he will show you which path to take."*)

"Wow!" I thought. "God not only reminds me to not give in to the fears that attack me all the time, but He provides guidance in exactly how to fight off the temptation to collapse into a mass of quivering, apprehensive flesh. How Satan must rejoice when he sees me rendered powerless to make wise choices and move in the direction of my glorious future. God promises that He has a great plan for my life (Jeremiah 29:11, *"For I know the plans I have for you," says the Lord. "They are plans for good and not for disaster, to give you a future and a hope."),* but if I'm too frightened to believe the Lord, what good does His promise do me?"

Suddenly, a picture flashed across my mind. I saw myself stripped free of all the fears that continually alarmed me, intimidating me into making foolish decisions. Instead I was boldly and confidently striding forward in life. I saw the smile on my face as I walked bravely along the pathways God had planned for me, and joyfully experienced all the blessings God had been waiting to pour into my life. My only regret was that I wasted so much of my life in the clutches of cowardice—better known as my "off the charts" fear factor!

----

1. What do you do if you see something happening that is wrong? Do you confront or keep quiet? Is that your default reaction or do you choose to do what God wants you to in each situation? Explain

_____
_____
_____
_____

2. On a scale of 0-10 where would you place your "fear factor?" Has this chapter changed your perception of exactly what your fear factor looks like and how strong it is? Why or why not? _____

_____
_____
_____

3. What percentage of the things you've feared has actually come true? What percentage of the things you've feared that DID come true was as bad or worse than you thought they'd be? What percentage of your time have you spent fearing these events or circumstances? How do you feel about spending that amount of time controlled by fear?

_____
_____
_____
_____

4. Were you surprised to find out that there are actually four known categories of fear? Which category includes your kind of fear? Do you feel like your fear is more understandable now that you know what it is? Explain _____

_____
_____
_____

5. Were you surprised to find that fear originates from our belief that God doesn't love us perfectly? Will that knowledge lessen the hold fear has on your emotions? Why or why not? _____

_____

_____

_____

6. Were you surprised to find out that the Bible is full of antidotes for your fear? Were any of them helpful to you? If so, give examples

_____

_____

_____

_____

7. Have you ever found yourself crippled and paralyzed by your fear? If so, give an example and describe what it felt like _____

_____

_____

_____

8. Were you surprised to find out that God is never the author of fear? How do you feel about allowing Satan the freedom to press your "fear" button whenever he wants to? Now that you have tools to use, describe, using a scale of 0-10, how hard you will fight back. Why? _____

_____

_____

_____

9. Can you picture yourself as a fearless, brave Christian striding through life doing God's will completely unhindered by fear? If so, what would that look like on a daily, detailed basis? _____

_____

_____

_____

Chapter 5

I HAVE TO BE GRATEFUL FOR **THAT**?

"God, no one has it as hard as I do," I grumbled. "I know you don't expect me to be grateful for THIS bad news. It hurts so badly, and the pain is more than I can bear. I've done nothing to deserve this level of pain, and I can't do anything to get rid of my torment, either. It's with me day and night, and I don't believe **anyone** could possibly be thankful in my situation."

"What's that you're saying, God?" I questioned incredulously. "You expect me to **be** thankful, and to **give** thanks verbally? That's crazy! I've never heard those rules before. What? You're insisting they're in the Bible?" I grabbed my Bible in disbelief flipping through the pages until I came to 1 Thessalonians 5:18, *"Be thankful in all circumstances, for this is God's will for you who belong to Christ Jesus."* I fell to the floor in shock with my head cradled between my knees. "God, you can't be serious!" I wailed. "I'm only human, and I'm telling you I can't be thankful for this wound. These circumstances will ruin my life! How can I be grateful for something that is so damaging to me?"

"You say you can make it turn out for my good?" I questioned, sure I had heard the Lord wrongly. "Where does it say that in the Bible?" I asked suspiciously. Immediately, Romans 8:28 came to my mind via the Lord's gentle prompting, *"And we know that God causes everything to work together for the good of those who love God and are called according to his purpose for them."*

"Okay, I read this promise, Lord, but how can you possibly make this heartache turn out for my good?" I asked with great skepticism. "Maybe

He's just talking about little problems," I reasoned. "Maybe He doesn't really mean 'everything'. And surely, He doesn't mean I have to be thankful in 'all circumstances.'" Convinced that I was right in my assessment of His words, I started to close my Bible when I felt prompted to look again. "Well, I'll look some more, but I won't believe Him unless He says it more than once," I thought, positive that this verse was one of a kind. "Only then will I be persuaded to believe the 'all' and the 'everything' words." Well, it wasn't long before I came across Ephesians 5:20, " . . . always giving thanks to God the Father for everything, in the name of our Lord Jesus Christ." There were those words again—"always" and "everything"! Right close by, I saw Philippians 4:4, "*Always be full of joy in the Lord. I say it again—rejoice!*"

"Wow! That verse sounds like a command," I thought, "not like just a nice thing to do if I feel like it." I read on to verse 6 in that chapter, "*Don't worry about anything; instead, pray about everything. Tell God what you need, and thank him for all he has done.*"

"Good grief!" I whined. "I can't even worry about anything. What AM I supposed to do with all these problems in my life?" Well, the Lord had an answer for that question, too, in Psalm 118:24, "*This is the day the LORD has made. We will rejoice and be glad in it.*"

"That's it?" I said incredulously. "I'm just supposed to 'rejoice and be glad' no matter what happens?" Not convinced yet because I couldn't believe I actually had to be thankful for my pain and loss, I made the mistake of looking further into the book of Psalms. With shock and bewilderment, I read verse after verse of how we're to be thankful for God's goodness, and to give praise continually. "That's impossible!" I shouted to the Lord. "No one in their right mind could be thankful for hard times. You're asking way too much of us humans." Suddenly, a new thought came to my mind. Just because the Bible said to be thankful in Psalms (that's the OLD Testament, after all), and just because Paul said it (He wasn't GOD) didn't mean Jesus said we had to be thankful. Positive that I was onto something, I quickly flipped through the pages of the gospels, only to find these words of Jesus, Himself, in Luke 6:20-23 "*God blesses you who are poor, for the Kingdom of God is yours. God blesses you who are hungry now, for you will be satisfied. God blesses you who weep now, for in due time you will laugh. What blessings await you when people hate you and exclude you and mock you and curse you as evil because you follow the Son of Man. When that happens, be happy! Yes, leap for joy! For a great reward awaits you in heaven.*" Slowly I began to close the Bible, completely out of options for my contention that maybe Jesus would understand how impossible it was to be grateful for my circumstances. If even He, who had lived on this earth and suffered terrible pain and injury, said I had to be thankful, I knew I had to at least consider the possibility of giving thanks in all things including my severe pain.

Ever the skeptic, though, I asked the Lord to show me ANYONE who was able to be thankful for their troubles, and He directed me to these verses in 2 Corinthians 1:3-11 where the apostle Paul was talking about his and his traveling companions' hardships and trials. In amazement I read about their experiences which were certainly worse than mine, and how joyfully they handled them. "*All praise to God, the Father of our Lord Jesus Christ. God is our merciful Father and the source of all comfort. He comforts us in all our troubles so that we can comfort others. When they are troubled, we will be able to give them the same comfort God has given us. For the more we suffer for Christ, the more God will shower us with his comfort through Christ. Even when we are weighed down with troubles, it is for your comfort and salvation! For when we ourselves are comforted, we will certainly comfort you. Then you can patiently endure the same things we suffer. We are confident that as you share in our sufferings, you will also share in the comfort God gives us. We think you ought to know, dear brothers and sisters, about the trouble we went through in the province of Asia. We were crushed and overwhelmed beyond our ability to endure, and we thought we would never live through it. In fact, we expected to die. But as a result, we stopped relying on ourselves and learned to rely only on God, who raises the dead. And he did rescue us from mortal danger, and he will rescue us again. We have placed our confidence in him, and he will continue to rescue us. And you are helping us by praying for us. Then many people will give thanks because God has graciously answered so many prayers for our safety.*" Wondering if Paul and his friends only praised God this one time, I went back to Acts to see if they ever thanked God in other hard situations. I came to Acts 16:19-25 where I read the story of men who

31

"grabbed Paul and Silas and dragged them before the authorities at the marketplace. 'The whole city is in an uproar because of these Jews!' they shouted to the city officials. 'They are teaching customs that are illegal for us Romans to practice.' A mob quickly formed against Paul and Silas, and the city officials ordered them stripped and beaten with wooden rods. They were severely beaten, and then they were thrown into prison. The jailer was ordered to make sure they didn't escape. So the jailer put them into the inner dungeon and clamped their feet in the stocks. Around midnight Paul and Silas were praying and singing hymns to God, and the other prisoners were listening." I slumped back in my chair realizing that God had answered every question I had about giving thanks in all things. He had said it time and time again in His word, and given me examples of real life people who had been thankful no matter what they had to endure (David fleeing from the wrath of King Saul, Daniel in the lion's den, Peter and John after being whipped). I knew I needed to accept the truth that I COULD give thanks in all things as promised in Philippians 4:13, *"For I can do everything through Christ, who gives me strength."*

I made one last plea to the Lord who never gets angry with His confused, fearful children. "Are there any blessings that come with the humanly impossible choice to be grateful no matter what happens to me?" I quavered. "If only I knew that the effort would be worth it, I think I could move forward to develop a grateful heart." Well, what do you know—He DOES offer rewards and blessings, and they're wonderful! The first one I found was in Colossians 3:15-17, *"And let the peace that comes from Christ rule in your hearts. For as members of one body you are called to live in peace. And always be thankful. Let the message about Christ, in all its richness, fill your lives. Teach and counsel each other with all the wisdom he gives. Sing psalms and hymns and spiritual songs to God with thankful hearts. And whatever you do or say, do it as a representative of the Lord Jesus, giving thanks through him to God the Father."* I noticed the theme of thankfulness and peace woven together and I realized that as I praise the Lord, peace enters my heart. I found that blessing reinforced in Philippians 4:6-7, *"Do not be anxious about anything, but in every situation, by prayer and petition, with thanksgiving, present your requests to God. And the peace of God, which transcends all understanding, will guard your hearts and your minds in Christ Jesus."* "I do crave peace," I told the Lord. "I'm sick of all the turmoil in my life, and if you can give me peace as I thank you for my circumstances, then I'm ready to start right now!"

As I searched for more blessings, I came across the verse in Nehemiah 8:10 where it says, *"Do not grieve, for the joy of the LORD is your strength."* I began to understand that if I praised and thanked the Lord, and chose to rejoice in every situation, God would give me strength to handle my pain. What a great blessing! Look at me—I'm already starting to praise the Lord and it wasn't hard at all when I think of all He's done for me and how good He's been to me. No wonder David said in Psalm 42:5, *"Why am I discouraged? Why is my heart so sad? I will put my hope in God! I will praise him again—."* Praise also keeps me from falling into the pits of hopelessness and despair, which is another incredible blessing. After logging many hours in those pits, I'm more than willing to practice my thankfulness toward the Lord.

Well, God wasn't done with the blessings for having a grateful heart yet. I found this verse in 1 Peter 1:6-7, *"So be truly glad. There is wonderful joy ahead, even though you have to endure many trials for a little while. These trials will show that your faith is genuine. It is being tested as fire tests and purifies gold—though your faith is far more precious than mere gold. So when your faith remains strong through many trials, it will bring you much praise and glory and honor on the day when Jesus Christ is revealed to the whole world."* Just think! If I choose to thank the Lord in all circumstances, my faith will grow stronger and stronger until I'm actually earning rewards for when I enter heaven. How cool is that? "I'm getting more excited about this praising idea, God, but what if I forget and start back into my whining and complaining mode? What did you say? You were aware that might happen so you had David write the Psalms which are full of reminders to praise the Lord? You think I should read Psalms as often as possible?" Shaking my head at how well God knows His children, and how perfectly He provides everything we need to obey Him, I knelt beside my bed, opened my broken heart, and by a forceful choice of my will, began thanking God for everything I could think of. Of course, you know what happened next! The more I thanked

Him, the more I thought of things to thank Him for until I had to get to my feet and start dancing for joy. God knew I'd feel that way if I'd "just do it," so He had David pen Psalm 30:11-12, "*You have turned my mourning into joyful dancing. You have taken away my clothes of mourning and clothed me with joy, that I might sing praises to you and not be silent. O Lord my God, I will give you thanks forever!*"

----

1. Have you ever wrestled with the command to give thanks in all things? If so, what did you do? _____

_____

_____

_____

2. Do you think God is asking too much of us to "rejoice always", or to give thanks in "all things"? Why or why not? Do you think there are times or circumstances that are too hard for any human to offer thanks for? Explain _____

_____

_____

_____

3. Can you think of other people in the Bible or in real life who gave thanks in horrific situations (i.e. Corrie Ten Boom, Joni Eareckson Tada)? Give some examples _____

_____

_____

_____

4. Were you surprised to know there are blessings that come our way when we thank God for hard times? Did that truth make you more likely to remember to be grateful instead of fearful or complaining? Why or why not? _____

_____

_____

_____

5. Describe any additional blessings you've discovered from intentionally praising the Lord even though it was desperately hard to do. _____

_____

_____

_____

Chapter 6

How Am I Supposed To Forgive When I Don't FEEL Like It?

I was screaming this question in my mind one morning as I struggled with my hurt feelings—once again! A family member continued to step on "my last nerve," and I was sick of it! "I know she does it on purpose," I exclaimed to myself, "So why should I forgive her and let her off the hook for her wrong behavior? She's rude, selfish, heartless, and just plain annoying. She should have to suffer some pain for the heartaches she's put me through!" Feeling justified in my assessment of the situation, I stood up, brushed my hands off symbolizing my feelings toward her, and proceeded to pick up my to-do list for the day.

As I perused the words on my list, suddenly they disappeared from my vision and I saw different words in my mind's eye—words from Scripture: *"Then Peter came to him and asked, 'Lord, how often should I forgive someone who sins against me? Seven times?' 'No, not seven times,' Jesus replied, 'but seventy times seven!'"* (Matthew 18:21-22). I raced for my Bible, not sure I was remembering Jesus' words correctly. "Surely, He was kidding or just using hyperbole to make a point," I assured myself. "He couldn't have been serious because that's not fair to me! Why should someone have the right to make my life miserable and then expect that I'll just forgive them? What's to keep them from doing the same thing over and over again? If my math is correct, He's telling me I have to forgive 490 times!! I can't do that!" My logic seemed so right to me that I almost closed my Bible before I saw what the rest of the chapter contained. The fact that the next verse jumped right into a story Jesus was telling caught my eye and I started to read it not realizing it had anything to do with forgiveness. *"Therefore, the Kingdom of Heaven can be compared to a king who decided to bring his accounts up to date with servants who had borrowed money from him. In the process, one of his debtors was brought in who owed him millions of dollars. He couldn't pay, so his master ordered that he be sold—along with his wife, his children, and everything he owned—to pay the debt. "But the man fell down before his master and begged him, 'Please, be patient with me, and I will pay it all.' Then his master was filled with pity for him, and he released him and forgave his debt. "But when the man left the king, he went to a fellow servant who owed him a few thousand dollars. He grabbed him by the throat and demanded instant payment. "His fellow servant fell down before him and begged for a little more time. 'Be patient with me, and I will pay it,' he pleaded. But his creditor wouldn't wait. He had the man arrested and put in prison until the debt could be paid in full. "When some of the other servants saw this, they were very upset. They went to the king and told him everything that had happened. Then the king called in the man he had forgiven and said, 'You evil servant! I forgave you that tremendous debt because you pleaded with me. Shouldn't you have mercy on your fellow servant, just as I had mercy on you?' Then the angry king sent the man to prison to be tortured until he had paid his entire debt. That's what my heavenly Father will do to you if you refuse to forgive your brothers and sisters from your heart."* (Matthew 18:23-35). "Ouch!" I thought, wincing at the harsh tone of the verses. "That doesn't sound like God is kidding around about forgiveness, or that it's just a nice thought. I wonder why He's so adamant that we forgive each other." Another verse popped into my head, *"If you forgive those who sin against you, your heavenly Father will forgive you. But if you refuse to forgive others, your Father will not forgive your sins."* Matthew 6:14-15. "Okay, I don't understand why God would be so harsh as to not forgive ME just because I can't find it in me to forgive my family member," I stewed. Furthermore, I thought God HAD to forgive in the sense that He couldn't HELP Himself because it's in His nature to forgive. Why would He link His behavior or limit His behavior based on mine, especially since He knows how to forgive so much easier than I do?" As my thoughts grew more and more frustrated, the idea came to me to look back at the story Jesus told. As I re-read it, I realized that the emphasis was on how huge a debt the king [Jesus] had forgiven for the servant. It was a debt he could never repay in several lifetimes, and his life was ruined as well as his family's lives because of this massive amount of money he owed. When he realized how destitute and hopeless his life was, he fell on his face and earnestly begged for mercy in a last-ditch effort to stave off disaster. It dawned on me that this story was a perfect picture of MY situation before a just God who is holy and sinless, and who demands perfection from his servants. I can never atone for my sins, nor can I ever hope to do enough to earn favor with God. I, too, was left with no choice but to cast myself on my face before Him and beg for His grace on my worthless life.

Suddenly, everything became clear to me! I had forgotten how huge my debt was, and how gloriously I had been forgiven for EVERYTHING! In fact, I had backslidden so far that I was no longer even moved by the goodness of the Lord or the incredible mercy He had shown me. To tell the truth, I had gone so far away from feeling gratitude toward the Lord that I was actually able to very cavalierly withhold forgiveness for the tiny offense of my family member compared to my enormous sin before the Lord. No wonder the king was so angry at his ungrateful servant! My prideful, arrogant heart was broken as I realized my sin in not racing to forgive my family member's slight as a way to honor the God who forgave me of so much. My tears fell fast and furious, and I sobbed with remorse as I begged God to give me another chance to practice His brand of forgiveness. I so desperately needed to be forgiven, I realized, as the enormity of my own sins passed before my eyes, and that means I definitely need to be attempting to forgive others.

"I just don't know how to forgive from my heart because my feelings won't cooperate," I wept to the Lord. He began to show me that forgiveness is not about feelings—it's about a choice of the will REGARDLESS of how I feel. Every time I have a bad thought about that person, I need to choose to forgive them. Every time they offend me, I need to choose to forgive them again and again. No wonder I need to be prepared to offer forgiveness 490 times to the same person! He assured me that the feelings would eventually follow, but I needed to start with a choice of my will.

God also showed me that I needed to forgive my family member for my OWN sake. When I questioned Him on how it would help **me,** He reminded me of the verse in Hebrews 12:15, "*Watch out that no poisonous root of bitterness grows up to trouble you, corrupting many.*" He showed me that by refusing to forgive, I would be tempted to hold a grudge which would lead to bitterness growing in my heart. Since I don't want to be a bitter, angry person (Who wants to be around THAT kind of person?), I shakily agreed to obey God's command. As I started to think of forgiving my family member, though, I found I was still struggling with how to do it. "Who have I ever seen forgiving someone who has deeply hurt them?" I mused. Suddenly a picture of Jesus on the cross scrolled across my mind. He said to people who were KILLING Him, "Father, forgive them because they don't know what they're doing."

"That's the key," I shouted! "They don't know what they're doing!" A feeling of excitement filled my heart when I realized that probably most people don't even KNOW they're being offensive and hurtful. "Perhaps that thought will help me approach this forgiveness process and be successful," I enthused. "Those Roman soldiers were just doing their jobs. They didn't know they were killing the Son of God! What if I made the assumption that my family member didn't realize how much she was hurting me? What if she's hurting, too, and doesn't know how to manage her pain?" Suddenly compassion and love for her poured through my heart, and I began to picture how much pain SHE must be feeling to hurt me like she has.

In the next minute, though, my fickle feelings began to change as I thought of forgiving her. "Why does she get off scot-free?" I grumbled. "Why do I have to do the forgiving and she doesn't have to change or be punished?" God, who is so faithful to help his struggling children, reminded me of His promise for this situation, "*Dear friends, never take revenge. Leave that to the righteous anger of God. For the Scriptures say, 'I will take revenge; I will pay them back,' says the LORD.*" (Romans 12:19). I realized that God is the perfect person to avenge my hurts since He knows the other person's heart and the best way to bring them to repentance. I quickly reminded myself, "If I just release that person into God's hands for His judgment to be carried out, I am set free of the sinful desire to mete out punishment or to withhold my love from that person. Those cravings will destroy me! If I let go, I will be able to focus fully on the business of forgiveness, secure in a God who sees my hurt and who will fight for me." What a relief! I raised my hands above my head as a symbol of offering my family member to the Lord, and pictured releasing her from my anger into His perfectly wise hands. I was shocked at the peace that flowed into my heart, and the cessation of my anger. The burden of tightly gripping my hurts fell off my tense shoulders and I felt light and free! Truly God knew what He was doing when He commanded us to forgive, even though that activity is one of the hardest I've ever engaged in.

----

1. Have you ever struggled to forgive someone? If so, who was it and why was it so hard? _____

_____

_____

_____

2. Does it seem easier to forgive a stranger than a family member? Why or why not? _____

_____

_____

_____

3. What was the hardest part of forgiving from the heart for you? Explain

_____

_____

_____

_____

4. Have you ever had to forgive someone 70 x 7? If so, how did that feel? Did you succeed? _____

_____

_____

_____

5. What has God had to forgive you of? Does that thought fill you with gratitude on a daily basis or do you find yourself forgetting about His mercy? _____

_____

_____

_____

6. Does your own sin make you more willing to forgive the sin of another against you? Why or why not? _____

_____

_____

_____

7. How do you feel about the idea of God taking vengeance on the person that hurt you? Are you able to trust Him in that area or do you believe your own punishment would be much better for that person? Explain _____

_____

_____

_____

8. Have you ever considered the golden rule to do unto others as you'd have them do unto you? Does that rule give you a different perspective or a more conservative approach to their punishment? Explain _____

_____

_____

_____

9. What do you think of the idea that forgiving someone starts in your will as opposed to your feelings? Does that thought help you begin the process of forgiving? Why or why not? _____

_____

_____

_____

Chapter 7

THE MOST UNRULY PART OF MY BODY!

"What do you mean I've offended you? I was just expressing my thoughts and feelings. You want me to be honest don't you?" I asked incredulously. "What's wrong with people?" I grumbled under my breath. "Honestly, some people are so sensitive! I have to walk on eggshells or they get their feelings hurt." As I walked away, I thought to myself, "Oh well, that's their problem, not mine." Suddenly I sensed the displeasure of the Lord over my attitude. "Why would He be upset with me?" I wondered. "I wasn't trying to hurt anyone." Remembrances began filling my mind of verses in the Bible talking about controlling my words, and with much trepidation, I began searching for them. "What if it IS my fault if my words offend someone," I worried. "What if I DO have to take full responsibility for everything that comes out of my mouth? What if God has given me a filter for my thoughts, and I haven't been using it?" Sure enough, James 3:1-12 was even harder to swallow than I remembered. God says, *"Dear brothers and sisters, not many of you should become teachers in the church, for we who teach will be judged more strictly. Indeed, we all make many mistakes. For if we could control our tongues, we would be perfect and could also control ourselves in every other way."* Just think! It's not our sexual drives, or food addictions, or even chemical addictions that God focuses on as the number one area for us to strive to control. It's our TONGUES! He says control of our tongues is the key to having mastery over the rest of our bodies because it's the most difficult part to rein in. He actually says if we could control our tongues we would be perfect! Ouch!! I guess I can't ever justify just "letting loose," or speaking my mind, or "letting it fly." Maybe God DOES hold me accountable for every word that comes out of my mouth as it says in Ephesians 4:29, *"Don't use foul or abusive language. Let everything you say be good and helpful, so that your words will be an encouragement to those who hear them."* The word "everything" is pretty all encompassing, isn't it?!

Well, God isn't finished yet—He goes on to say, *"We can make a large horse go wherever we want by means of a small bit in its mouth. And a small rudder makes a huge ship turn wherever the pilot chooses to go, even though the winds are strong. In the same way, the tongue is a small thing that makes grand speeches."* So much good can be done with our tongues. They are a wonderful part of our bodies and we should be very thankful for their potential to do enormous Kingdom good. As with anything that incredible, though, there is equal potential for our tongues to do unspeakable harm. God is so strong and graphic in His description of the evil side of our tongues. *"But a tiny spark can set a great forest on fire. And the tongue is a flame of fire. It is a whole world of wickedness, corrupting your entire body. It can set your whole life on fire, for it is set on fire by hell itself."* "Surely God is kidding, or maybe just using exaggeration to make a point," I thought. "It can't be THAT bad . . ." Just then my mind filled with memories of the hurtful, destructive words that have been said to me, and how they wreaked havoc on my self-esteem. I writhed anew in the anguish I still felt at those awful words raining down on my vulnerable heart. And then, much to my shame, I remembered the times I had said hateful words out of anger or a desire to actually destroy someone I was threatened by. I saw the slump of their shoulders as I hurled my best shots at them, the tears that filled their eyes, the hopelessness in their faces, and I rejoiced at their suffering! I began to realize that God wasn't kidding—He was dead serious about the destructive nature of our tongues.

God finishes that part of James 3 by saying, *"People can tame all kinds of animals, birds, reptiles, and fish, but no one can tame the tongue. It is restless and evil, full of deadly poison. Sometimes it praises our Lord and Father, and sometimes it curses those who have been made in the image of God. And so blessing and cursing come pouring out of the same mouth. Surely, my brothers and sisters, this is not right! Does a spring of water bubble out with both fresh water and bitter water? Does a fig tree produce olives, or a grapevine produce figs? No, and you can't draw fresh water from a salty spring."* Much to my shock, as I read and re-read these verses, I realized God is saying that our tongues can't actually speak both good and evil because that would mean both Satan and God can reside equally in our hearts at the same time. God says, *"If we claim to have fellowship with him yet walk in the darkness, we lie and do not live by the truth."* I John 1:6. One or the other has to be at the controls of our lives—not both. If God has taken up residence in our hearts, Satan should be on his way out more and more each day. Our tongues should then reflect this truth by speaking more and more of God's truths and less and less of Satan's lies.

"Okay," I said to myself—after all I can't argue with this passage since it's incredibly clear in its teaching, "I understand that I have to control my urges to use my words as weapons, but I didn't mean to hurt this person. I just wasn't thinking about how I was coming across." God, who won't ever let me off the hook, reminded me of the verse in Matthew 12:36, *"But I tell you that every careless word that people speak, they shall give an accounting for it in the day of judgment."* I was shocked! "How would anyone ever dare to speak, then," I groused. It seemed impossible to please the Lord with my words! I quickly found out that God has a sense of humor because He directed my eyes to this verse in James 1:19, *"Understand this, my dear brothers and sisters: You must all be quick to listen, slow to speak, and slow to get angry."* "Fine!" I said with poor grace. "I understand that I just have to keep my mouth shut if I don't want to sin, or at least run my words past Him before I dare speak! How do I remember to do that, though, and how will I know if I accidentally offend someone?" Of course the perfect verse, well actually it's a prayer, came to my mind, *"May the words of my mouth and the meditation of my heart be pleasing to you, O LORD, my rock and my redeemer."* Psalm 19:14. I noticed that while the Lord wants me to pray for help in making my words please Him, He also includes the need to pray about the topics I allow my mind to feed on which is where my words originate from. As hard a choice as it is to ask God to guide and bless my thoughts and my conversation, I desperately want to be as close to perfect in God's eyes as possible, and it appears that the only way to achieve my goal is to let HIM control my tongue!

\-

1. Have you ever offended someone by something you said or the way you said it? How did you discern that there was an offense? Were you shocked at the knowledge you had offended someone? _____

_____

_____

_____

2. Once you realized you had offended someone, how did you handle that offense? What was the result? _____

_____

_____

_____

3. Is it ever the other person's fault if they are offended by something you say? Is there such a thing as being too sensitive? Is there ever a time when it's okay to walk away from someone's offense believing it's not your fault? Explain _____

_____

_____

_____

4. On a scale of 0-10 how well do you control your tongue? How would your friends/co-workers rate you on this scale? Would you be willing to ask them? _____

_____

_____

_____

5. Why do you think God is so strong on cautioning us against jumping too quickly into becoming teachers in the church? Have you ever led a small group, or been in a position to be a role model, or been in a leadership position? What do you think of the fact that you will be judged more strictly? _____

_____

_____

_____

6. Do you think teachers ever have negative, superior, or condescending thoughts while teaching a class? (i.e. I'm glad I'm in control! Now I get the chance to scold that person without naming names! I can use my position as a platform or a soapbox. Look how important I am – everyone listens to me and does whatever I tell them to, etc.) Have you ever sensed any of those thoughts influencing a teacher, or actually had it happen to you? How did you handle that scenario? On a scale of 0 – 10, how tempting would it be for you to use a position as a teacher/trainer/role model to gain a following, or to live for praise, or to seek for glory and fame, or to be thought of as holy, or to develop an attitude as a know-it-all? Explain

_____

_____

_____

_____

7. What do you think of God's words about the tongue, *"It can set your whole life on fire, for it is set on fire by hell itself."* Do you think it's true of your tongue? If so, give an example of when your tongue got you in major trouble? _____

_____

_____

_____

8. On a scale of 0-10, what percentage of words coming off your tongue are positive? Do you think you're an encourager or a discourager? How do you think that affects your ability to be "perfect" in God's eyes? What will you do to raise your score? _____

_____

_____

_____

9. What do you think of the verse that tells us to be *"quick to listen, slow to speak, and slow to get angry?"* What percentage of the time do you listen versus speaking? What would help you increase your listening ability and what hinders you from listening? _____

_____

_____

_____

10. What do you think of the idea of praying over your words before speaking them? Is that realistic? Is it important? What changes might occur in your life if you actually asked God *"May the words of my mouth and the meditation of my heart be pleasing to you, O LORD?"* _____

_____

_____

_____

Chapter 8

WHY DO I HAVE TO APOLOGIZE?
CAN'T I JUST DO BETTER NEXT TIME?

"Come on Lord," I whined. "You know I didn't mean to offend that person. You know I'm just too busy and stressed out to be careful what I say and how I say it. Besides, you know that this person is just too sensitive! She needs to move on and get over herself." I was sure my explanation would satisfy the Lord because He knows all the pressure I'm under. It's not like I'm a bad person! He needs to give me more strength and patience if He wants me to be all soft and lovey-dovey and positive. It's not my fault there's so much on my plate. Convinced that I was in the right, I brushed off my feelings of guilt and started to resume my frenetic pace of life.

As time went on, I began to notice that I didn't feel as close to the Lord as I did in the past. My prayers didn't seem to ascend much past the ceiling. I was going through the motions of trying to be a good Christian, serving at church, reaching out to the destitute, giving of my time and resources, but nothing brought me any real peace and joy. My irritation and impatience with those around me seemed to grow, and I found myself offending people right and left. The worst part was that my ability to really love people with God's kind of love seemed to shrivel up and die right before my eyes! All I could see were all their faults and failures which made me even more frustrated and upset with people, my job, my family, and yes, even life itself.

One day, in a fit of frustration and despair, I actually asked the Lord to show me what was wrong in my heart. "Where are the peace, joy, contentment, and soul satisfaction you promised?" I asked angrily. "This

Christian life is not what I signed up for!" As I waited on my knees, not really expecting an answer but too discouraged to get up and go on, I remembered this verse in James 5:16, *"Confess your sins to each other and pray for each other so that you may be healed. The earnest prayer of a righteous person has great power and produces wonderful results."* "Why are you reminding me of this verse?" I demanded of the Lord. "I don't have any sins I need to confess, and I'm not sick! What do I need to be healed of?" God gently began reminding me of my refusal to apologize to those I'd offended. As I started to bristle, He asked me to look at my words and behavior from the other person's point of view. "How would YOU have handled being talked to like that or treated like that?" He whispered deep in my heart. I resisted His voice at first because it was too hard and painful to see myself from another person's point of view. Then His whisper came again, "Would you have said or done those things if I were standing right there in your sight?" My defenses crumbled. Suddenly, I realized that I was blaming others for their hurt feelings instead of dealing with my wrong attitude, behavior, and words. Finally I was ready to say, "What do you want me to do, Lord?" and mean it with all my heart.

Immediately, the Lord brought another verse to my mind: *"Humble yourselves, therefore, under God's mighty hand, that he may lift you up in due time."* (James 4:10). "I **hate** those words, 'humble yourselves,'" I muttered to myself. "I'm afraid the other person will take advantage of me if I do that, or will think they won, or will use my humbleness to make fun of me." God reminded me that the alternative would be hardness in my heart and the inability to really love Him or anyone else, AND the loss of any rewards in Heaven reducing me to a pauper. As I reviewed my two choices, I finally gave in to the loving insistence of the Lord, and dropped to my knees. "Okay, Lord," I sighed. "I'll do whatever you show me to do, but please protect me and give me the strength to follow you no matter how I'm treated or scorned."

As I rose on my shaky legs, full of fear, but with a new resolve in my heart, the Lord brought to my attention the name of the person I had offended the most grievously. "Not her," I begged desperately. "Can't I start out with someone easy, so I get practice first?" The Lord showed me that I would lose my momentum if I didn't start with the hardest person first, so I gave in to His gentle prompting and pulled out my phone. As I waited through the ringing, I prayed that the person would be gone and I could leave a message, or that I would die on the spot and not have to go through with this humbling business. When the person answered the phone, I gathered my courage and said, "I know I offended you, but I didn't know you would be so sensitive." The other person shouted at me in anger and hung up on me! "What did I do wrong, Lord?" I quavered, shaken up by the other person's volatility. The Lord reminded me that I needed to be humble and confess my sins to this person. With much fear and trepidation, I dialed the number again, quivering in my boots. Again, the person answered, but with a much greater sense of resistance toward me. Hesitantly, I started in again with my apology. "I know I was wrong in what I said to you and how I treated you, but I was having a bad day. You have no idea how much stress I have in my life." The person on the other end of the phone listened silently and then hung up on me again. "Lord, what am I doing wrong!" I shouted in frustration. "I'm really trying here."

"Have you truly humbled yourself?" I heard the Lord whisper. "You mean I have to go even lower?" I exclaimed in frustration. "Fine," I mumbled, and picked up the phone again. This time I said with as much sincerity as I could muster, "I was wrong in what I said and did to you." I waited a moment and then the temptation was too great to resist, and I reminded them of their own fault in the situation, too. "After all, if I have to humble myself, they need to be humbled, as well," I reasoned. "Why should I have to take ALL the blame?" Well, for the third time the phone was slammed down in my ear after I was totally reamed out. "Okay, God," I said in despair. "This apology thing is not working. I've done my best and looked what happened. Things are worse now than they were before I called!" God, who is so patient with me, explained once again that I needed to completely humble myself no matter what it cost me. He reminded me that the other person's wrong-doings were none of my business, and that I needed to leave their behavior up to Him to deal with. I was only responsible to own my own faults. As I lay face down before the Lord as humbled as possible, I began to see my faults from the other person's perspective, and they looked ugly. Guilt and sorrow began to pour over me as I saw my offense through God's eyes. As I picked up the phone with trembling hands, tears were pouring down my face. I could hardly get the words out when the "hello" came over the phone. "I was so wrong in how I treated you," I sobbed. "I have no excuse for my hurtful behavior, and I'm really sorry for the pain I caused you. I pray you can find it in your heart to forgive me, and I promise I'll do everything in my power to make things right." My humble words were met by silence which stretched on and on. I didn't know what to do next, but I sensed the Lord telling me to just wait. Finally I heard soft words over the phone, "I do forgive you, but I don't know if I can trust you again." "I understand," I responded. "I will take as long as I need to prove to you that, with God's help, I can be trusted."

As I got off the phone, I checked myself for any bruises or injuries and found NONE! Instead, I was flooded with the peace that comes from obedience to the Lord even when I didn't want to comply with His commands. I began to realize that while obedience is hard, the rewards are well worth it in the end—peace, joy, and a clear conscience! I also understood that because it was so hard to humble myself, and so embarrassing to have to apologize, this exercise would be the very thing that would force me to think before I spoke in the future. Since I hated having to apologize the correct way, taking full responsibility for my behavior with no excuses or blame, I would be so careful going forward not to give offense in any way, shape, or form. I would also be much quicker to sense when I HAVE offended someone, and to make things right as soon as possible. I desperately wanted to be at peace with the Lord and everyone else instead of being filled with guilt and defensiveness. I made the commitment at that point to follow the words of John C. Maxwell, "**A man must be big enough to admit his mistakes, smart enough to profit from them, and strong enough to correct them**." May God help me adopt His words in 1 Corinthians 10:32 as my motto: "*Don't give offense to Jews or Gentiles or the church of God.*"

----

1. What do you think of the idea of apologizing? Do you think it's critical to a healthy Christian life, or are you more in the mindset of "Loving someone means never having to say you're sorry?" Explain _____

_____

_____

_____

2. Do you think problems can usually solve themselves if you just ignore them and act like nothing is wrong? Why or why not? Have you ever seen that approach work? If so, give an example _____

_____

_____

_____

3. What do you think of the idea that there could be a right and a wrong way to handle an apology? Have you ever received one where the person kind of, sort of took blame, but made sure to include you in the fault-finding? If so, describe how that kind of an apology made you feel?

_____

_____

_____

_____

4. Has there ever been a time where you could say you were 100% right in a relational blow-up? Has there ever been a time when you were 100% at fault? If either of these statements is true, give examples _____

_____

_____

_____

5. Do you find it hard to apologize, and to do it the correct way? If so, why is it so hard? _____

_____

_____

_____

6. Have you ever apologized in one of the incorrect ways? If so, what was the end result? _____

_____

_____

_____

7. Since Jesus never sinned, we have no situation in the Bible showing Him apologizing correctly so we have to look at others. Have you ever seen another person apologize correctly, or been the recipient of a loving, gracious, heart-felt apology? If so, how did you feel, and how did you respond? _____

_____

_____

_____

8. Have you ever seen benefits come to you from apologizing correctly? If so, describe them _____

_____

_____

_____

9. After apologizing correctly and regaining your peace, joy, and clear conscience, have you ever felt Satan wheedling his way back into your thoughts because you felt so vulnerable and exposed? If so, what did you do about it? Would it be helpful to be on guard for Satan's lies? Fear and bitterness could be some of his tricks—can you think of any others?

_____

_____

_____

_____

Chapter 9

Loving Others Is For The Birds!

"Lord, it's impossible to love others! I've tried and tried and all I get for my efforts is another slap in the face. I know You command us to love each other ("*So now I am giving you a new commandment: Love each other. Just as I have loved you, you should love each other.*" John 13:34), but I'm starting to think that attempting to love other people is the equivalent of banging my head against the wall. It brings no positive results and it only hurts me in the end. I know, I know—practice the Golden Rule, 'Do unto others as you would have others do unto you,' but I've tried and it doesn't work! I love backrubs so I tried to give my friend a backrub when she was stressed out, and she shouted at me, 'Stop touching me! I don't like being touched.' Another time I did the laundry for a friend that was going through hard times, and then cleaned her house for her. Not only was she not grateful, she was very upset because I didn't do things the way SHE wanted them done. I'm sorry, Lord, but I'm sick of getting berated, beat-up, castigated, reprimanded, reproached, and vilified for trying to show love!" I got up off my knees, wiped the tears from my face, and began getting ready for the day. "I hate it when the Lord asks me to do things that are impossible," I muttered to myself knowing that I was in for a bad day.

Later, during my lunch break, I went to sit in the park and enjoy the sunny day. I brought my Bible along because I was determined to get to the bottom of this "love others" issue. I knew God was serious about the topic of love because He devoted so many verses in His Word to this subject. I turned to 1 John 2 and began reading random verses, amazed at the intensity of the words used. He says in verses 7-11, *"Dear friends, I am not writing a new commandment for you; rather it is an old one you have had from the very beginning. This old commandment—to love one another—is the same message you heard before. Yet it is also new. Jesus lived the truth of this commandment, and you also are living it. For the darkness is disappearing, and the true light is already shining. If anyone claims, 'I am living in the light,' but hates a Christian brother or sister, that person is still living in darkness. Anyone who loves another brother or sister is living in the light and does not cause others to stumble. But anyone who hates another brother or sister is still living and walking in darkness. Such a person does not know the way to go, having been blinded by the darkness."*

"Okay, so those are pretty harsh words," I mused, "but surely they don't apply to ME. I don't HATE anyone—I just don't like certain people, or the way they treat me. I just want to push them out of my life and not have to deal with them. I don't want to see them DEAD or even badly hurt. I just hope someday someone hurts them like they've hurt me so they can see what it feels like." Convinced that I was absolved of any guilt, I read on only to be brought up short in 1 John 3:11-20, *"This is the message you have heard from the beginning: We should love one another. We must not be like Cain, who belonged to the evil one and killed his brother. And why did he kill him? Because Cain had been doing what was evil, and his brother had been doing what was righteous. So don't be surprised, dear brothers and sisters, if the world hates you. If we love our Christian brothers and sisters, it proves that we have passed from death to life. But a person who has no love is still dead. Anyone who hates another brother or sister is really a murderer at heart. And you know that murderers don't have eternal life within them. We know what real love is because Jesus gave up his life for us. So we also ought to give up our lives for our brothers and sisters. If someone has enough money to live well and sees a brother or sister in need but shows no compassion—how can God's love be in that person? Dear children, let's not merely say that we love each other; let us show the truth by our actions. Our actions will show that we belong to the truth, so we will be confident when we stand before God."*

"What!" I shrieked, quickly covering my mouth when I remembered I was in a public park. "I don't even LIKE these people. Why would I give up my life for them? That doesn't make any sense. Well, maybe I would give up my life for my best friend or for my kids, but certainly not for those people who've hurt me so deeply. What's that you're saying, Lord? You gave up your life for your ENEMIES? You expect me to do the same? Where does it say that in the Bible?" Of course, by now, I should know better than to argue with the Lord because I found these verses in Romans 5:7-8, 10, *"Now, most people would not be willing to die for an upright person, though someone might perhaps be willing to die for a person who is especially good. But God showed his great love for us by sending Christ to die for us while we were still sinners. For since our friendship with God was restored by the death of his Son while we were still his enemies, we will certainly be saved through the life of his Son."* Horrified at the thought that maybe I was wrong, and I DID need to love my enemies, I begged God to show me anywhere in His Word where He said I had to act loving to hurtful people just because HE did. Much to my shock and consternation, I found these verses which were so clear and understandable that I had nothing left to argue about. Matthew 5:43-48 says, *"You have heard the law that says, 'Love your neighbor' and hate your enemy. But I say, love your enemies! Pray for those who persecute you! In that way, you will be acting as true children of your Father in heaven. For he gives his sunlight to both the evil and the good, and he sends rain on the just and the unjust alike. If you love only those who love you, what reward is there for that? Even corrupt tax collectors do that much. If you are kind only to your friends, how are you different from anyone else? Even pagans do that. But you are to be perfect, even as your Father in heaven is perfect."*

Now I didn't care who heard me and saw me! I was so distraught that I fell to my knees in front of the park bench wailing and moaning in anguish over the thought of opening myself up again to being hurt over and over. As I huddled in a miserable heap, forgetting that I had a job to get back to, forgetting that the ground was wet, and not caring about anything except my need to understand how God expected me to do the impossible at my own risk, I suddenly became aware of the presence of the Lord! The great God of the Universe was willing to bring insight into my troubled heart through His gentle whispers. Little by little, I began to understand that the key to obeying God's command was my MOTIVES! WHY was I doing the "loving" things I was doing? Was I being an enabler? While the word "enable" has only positive connotations (give power, means, competence, or ability to; authorize, to make possible or easy, to make ready; equip), the word "enabler" has come to mean something negative. One definition sums up an enabler this way: "Doing for others what they should be doing for themselves." I realized that if I did nice things for others allowing them to become lazy or selfish, I wasn't actually loving them. I was, instead, doing something very hurtful to them. I groaned aloud at all the times I remembered doing things for others just to help them out, or just to be nice, when they should have been forced to do those things for themselves. Because I was always bailing them out, or picking up the pieces, or trying to keep them out of trouble, I was robbing them of lessons they needed to learn. What I thought were acts of love turned out to be just the opposite!

As I was reeling from this first revelation, a second one followed closely behind. Guilt! I shuddered to think of how many times I had acted in loving ways out of pure guilt. I knew I was supposed to do the loving thing, and that it was expected of me. Hey, I even expected it of myself! "Any decent person, let alone a Christian, would take a meal to a hurting family, or offer to clean the house of a newly divorced friend, or willingly do the laundry of a mom who just had a baby," I would admonish myself. "Now just go do it!" And so I trudged off to do my kind, loving works with a disgruntled attitude carefully hidden behind a bright, cheerful smile. Now I saw myself with new eyes and the picture was pretty awful!

Well, the Lord wasn't done with me yet. He began to show me other motives I had that were hindering my desire to love as He loves. I suddenly could remember times when I had manipulated people to do what I wanted them to do. While none of my abhorrent actions were done consciously, I realized that in my subconscious mind, I still knew what I was doing. I gave people desperately needed money hoping they would put in a good word for me at the office. I did nice things for others hoping they would give ME money. I became friends with acquaintances hoping they would introduce me to more sought after people. I offered to babysit my friends' kids hoping they would return the favor two or three times for every time I volunteered. I offered love hoping that people would overlook the faults in my life that I didn't want to deal with. The ugliness of my motives overwhelmed me and my head sank lower and lower onto the park bench. "How could I have thought using people was the same as loving them?" I lamented. "I wonder if people KNEW what I was doing and felt controlled by me. Maybe THAT'S why I got so many negative responses to my attempts to be "loving."

A new thought came quickly on the heels of understanding my manipulating motives. What about my selfish motives? Many times I've been loving and helpful to make me feel better about myself. "Look at me," I'd think. "I'm a really good Christian. I wonder if everyone else is noticing. Maybe I'll be more sought after. Maybe I'll be looked up to and listened to. Maybe I'll be asked to lead a group. I'm sure even God is noticing my good deeds and they'll be counted as great treasure in Heaven. YUCK!" In my despair over the ugliness in my heart, I put my head in my hands and begged the Lord to forgive me. I couldn't stand the sight of my ego needing so desperately to be stroked, and my selfishness driving me to manipulate and control people in the name of love. I saw that I was willing to do anything for others as long as I gained some benefit from it. Wondering if God could ever forgive my sinful ways, I dragged myself back to work, wet knees, red eyes, and all.

Later that evening, I allowed all the thoughts to surface that I had been suppressing since lunch time. "God, do you hate me?" I sobbed. "I'm so sinful and wrong in everything I say and do! You don't hate me? You already knew how sinful I am? You even put a verse in the Bible about my sinful heart?" Clutching at hope, I grabbed my Bible and turned to Jeremiah 17:9, "*The human heart is the most deceitful of all things, and desperately wicked. Who really knows how bad it is?*" Amazed at God's ability to put His finger on exactly what the problem was and to still love me knowing the extent of my sin, I pleaded with Him to forgive me and to show me how to love as He loves. I turned to the "Love Chapter"—1 Corinthians 13, and began to study it for clues. I found absolutely impossible descriptions of love, and I became more morose as I read them. Verses 4-7 say, "*Love is patient and kind. Love is not jealous or boastful or proud or rude. It does not demand its own way. It is not irritable, and it keeps no record of being wronged. It does not rejoice about injustice but rejoices whenever the truth wins out. Love never gives up, never loses faith, is always hopeful, and endures through every circumstance."*

"God," I whined. "I can't do these things you're asking of me. They're just too hard! Let's just start with 'Love is patient and kind!' Who in the world can ever fulfill those two words, let alone all the other descriptions? What did you say, Lord?" I asked incredulously, certain I had heard the Lord wrongly. "You're saying I CAN do those things? Oh yeah, 'I can do all things through Christ who gives me strength.'" (Philippians 4:13). "Okay, God, can I completely trust that You will come through for me in the strength area? Some of these people are hard to love and they intimidate me! I feel like a puppy that's been accidently kicked one too many times, and only wants to slink away into a corner." Since I heard no response to my presumptuous question, I picked up my Bible and was shocked to read this verse in Romans 8:32, "*Since he did not spare even his own Son but gave him up for us all, won't he also give us everything else?*" Understanding flooded into my soul! How could I have even ASKED a question like that when God had already given me His most prized possession? I realized that giving me strength was just a drop in the bucket compared to giving me His own Son. Greatly relieved that all of God's strength was available to help me show love according to His will, I still held back, worried that I wouldn't know exactly what love looked like. After all, I had gotten used to loving with ulterior motives. How would I know what REAL love looked like? Besides, God Himself said my heart was deceitful and that I wouldn't even know if I had wrong motives. Flipping through more pages in my Bible, I found this verse, "*If you need wisdom, ask our generous God, and he will give it to you. He will not rebuke you for asking.*" (James 1:5) Relief flooded over me as I realized God had all the bases covered! He would give strength AND wisdom if I was willing to show love His way.

Finally I was open to hearing God's voice on how He wanted me to love people. He prompted me to search His Word some more and I came across Philippians 2:3, "*Don't be selfish; don't try to impress others. Be humble, thinking of others as better than yourselves.*" Immediately, I begged the Lord to show me whenever selfishness or my ego were in the way of portraying God's love. I also had no idea I had to humble myself in order to love others and to view them as better than myself, but it made sense! I hate it when I feel like others are trying to impress me, or when they can't be bothered to listen to anything I have to say. Now I was really excited, sure I was onto the truth of God's form of love. The next verse I found gave more clues. Romans 12:10 says, "*Be devoted to one another in love. Honor one another above yourselves.*"

"Wow!" I thought. "I'm to be devoted to others which means to be 'zealous or ardent in attachment, loyalty, or affection.' I've never thought of those kinds of emotions being part of true love. I'm also to honor others, even above myself, and my time constraints, and what I'd prefer to do, which means to hold them in 'high respect.'" As I pondered these words, I realized that I would LOVE to have others treat me that way. "AHA!" I thought to myself. "THAT'S what the Golden Rule means! I'm to focus on others, listening to them, watching them, and taking mental notes until I KNOW what they would consider loving acts coming from me." I remembered a book by Dr. Gary Chapman called "The Five Love Languages." In it the author described how various expressions of love (words of affirmation, acts of service, quality time, receiving gifts, physical touch) affect each of us differently in our love receptors. I appreciate getting backrubs, but my friend felt awkward and uncomfortable when people touched her which caused her negative reaction. She had a different love language. I bounced on my chair excitedly as understanding flooded my heart. I had to prove to others that I really did care about them by being willing to share their pain with them even if I didn't understand it, to embrace their joy even if it made no sense to me, and to share their visions even though my own visions were far different—just like I would want to be treated. In other words, I had to be willing to join them in their "pits" and to stand on their mountaintops with them (*"Be happy with those who are happy, and weep with those who weep.*" Romans 12:15) which is exactly what the Lord does in showing His love to me.

Another verse, Galatians 5:26, gave me some insight into what I have to remove from my heart in order to love well, "*Let us not become conceited, provoking and envying each other."* Any negative feelings toward others, any desire to compete or compare myself with others, and any remnants of pride need to be brought under the light of the Holy Spirit so He can clean them away. One more verse summed up the way I was to react to everyone around me, *"Since God chose you to be the holy people he loves, you must clothe yourselves with tenderhearted mercy, kindness, humility, gentleness, and patience."* (Colossians 3:12). I realized it was a CHOICE I had to make each day to be Christ-like in my love no matter how I felt, and that the Lord would give me the strength to actually be sincere . . . to ALL people . . . no matter HOW I viewed the person . . . no matter HOW they treated me . . . no matter how anyone ELSE treated that person. The Lord's perspective and guidance were all that mattered, and if He prompted me to acts of kindness, I was to DO them! If He put a restraining hand on my heart, I was to hold back on those acts of service no matter how desperately I thought they were needed. Following that plan would deal with my motives being out of whack, too! "I got it, Lord," I sighed in relief, sure that my "love" life would flow much more smoothly now. Just as I closed my Bible, the doorbell rang. When I looked out the peephole, my heart sank! "Lord, what should I do?" I panicked. "It's my nosy neighbor who continually looks for ways to put me down." As I reached for the doorknob, I thought I heard the Lord whisper in my ear, "Not everyone responded well to my overtures of love, either, even though they were always perfectly given." With a smile on my face that was pretty close to sincere, I opened the door ready to embark on this love fest with none other than the Lover of my soul.

----

1. Have you ever tried to love someone and they misunderstood your motives and threw your attempts back in your face? If so, how did that feel? Are you still open to loving others? Explain _____

_____

_____

_____

2. How do you feel about God's command to love others just as He has loved us? Explain _____

_____

_____

_____

3. Have you ever loved with wrong motives? If so, what were your motives? How well did they serve you? Give an example _____

_____

_____

_____

4. What percentage of time do you spend loving others in the same way **you** would want to have love shown to you (ex. Giving backrubs because that's what I like)? Explain _____

_____

_____

_____

5. What percentage of time do you spend studying the other person until you can show them love the way THEY want to have it shown? Explain _____

_____

_____

_____

6. How do you feel about having to always ask the Lord HOW to show love to each person in your world and WHEN to show it? What percentage of time do you ask him versus the amount of times you just do what feels right at the moment? Could you possibly be hurting people in your attempts to love them? Why or why not? _____

_____

_____

_____

7. Describe as honestly as possible how the Lord loves you on a daily basis. How do you feel about His way of loving you? Give an example

_____

_____

_____

_____

Chapter 10

But I *Deserve* A Good Life— I'm An American!

"Lord," I cried. "Why are these bad things happening to me? What have I done to deserve them? I've tried to follow you and look where it's gotten me—nothing but trouble! What good does it do to serve You if there are no benefits in it for me? I'm in debt, my marriage is in shambles, my kids aren't following you like I thought they would, I don't like my job, and my church is a big disappointment. This kind of life is NOT what I signed up for when I became a Christian! I thought you promised that if I did things Your way you would bless me and make my ways prosper?" I sat on the edge of my bed filled with despair. Somewhere along the way God had let me down, and I didn't know where to go from here. I'd tried running my own life, and that didn't work out very well which was why I turned to God. Now that HE proved untrustworthy, I didn't know where else to turn.

Slowly, I pulled myself together to face another rotten day when I noticed my neglected Bible sticking out from under the edge of my bed. I picked it up wondering if I should just throw it in the trash or if there might still be some hope for me between its pages. Much to my shock and dismay, my Bible fell open to the book of Proverbs and I read verses like these, "*No harm comes to the godly, but the wicked have their fill of trouble.*" (12:21), "*There is treasure in the house of the godly, but the earnings of the wicked bring trouble.*" (15:6), and, "*The blessing of the Lord makes a person rich, and he adds no sorrow with it.*" (10:22). "What do these verses mean?" I wailed in desperation. "Are you saying, Lord, that

I'm not a godly person? I certainly have no "treasure" or riches, and harm has definitely come my way!" Convinced now that I had no value or worth to the Lord and that I must have sinned in some grievous way, I found myself reading Deuteronomy 28:1-13 and sinking further and further into despondency, *"If you fully obey the Lord your God and carefully keep all his commands that I am giving you today, the Lord your God will set you high above all the nations of the world. You will experience all these blessings if you obey the Lord your God: Your towns and your fields will be blessed. Your children and your crops will be blessed. The offspring of your herds and flocks will be blessed. Your fruit baskets and breadboards will be blessed. Wherever you go and whatever you do, you will be blessed. The Lord will conquer your enemies when they attack you. They will attack you from one direction, but they will scatter from you in seven! The Lord will guarantee a blessing on everything you do and will fill your storehouses with grain. The Lord your God will bless you in the land he is giving you. "If you obey the commands of the Lord your God and walk in his ways, the Lord will establish you as his holy people as he swore he would do. Then all the nations of the world will see that you are a people claimed by the Lord, and they will stand in awe of you. The Lord will give you prosperity in the land he swore to your ancestors to give you, blessing you with many children, numerous livestock, and abundant crops. The Lord will send rain at the proper time from his rich treasury in the heavens and will bless all the work you do. You will lend to many nations, but you will never need to borrow from them. If you listen to these commands of the Lord your God that I am giving you today, and if you carefully obey them, the Lord will make you the head and not the tail, and you will always be on top and never at the bottom."*

"I don't understand," I complained to the Lord. "Do I have to be a farmer before you bless me? I don't remember seeing lots of wealthy farmers, come to think of it, but nothing else makes sense to me." Assuming I'd hear nothing back from the Lord in response to my lamenting, I began to close my Bible, only to sense the Lord moving my fingers in the direction of the New Testament. Curiosity overcame my self-pity, and I began to wonder what Jesus had to say on this whole topic of blessings for the godly versus punishment for the sinful. Much to my surprise, Jesus' words are in direct contrast to what I was reading in the Old Testament! He says, "*I have told you all this so that you may have peace in me. Here on earth you will have many trials and sorrows. But take heart, because I have overcome the world.*" (John 16:33). He goes on to say something contrary to anything I had ever heard before, "*The world would love you as one of its own if you belonged to it, but you are no longer part of the world. I chose you to come out of the world, so it hates you. Do you remember what I told you? 'A slave is not greater than the master.' Since they persecuted me, naturally they will persecute you. And if they had listened to me, they would listen to you. They will do all this to you because of me, for they have rejected the One who sent me.*" (John 15:20). Since Matthew 8:20 says, "*But Jesus replied, 'Foxes have dens to live in, and birds have nests, but the Son of Man has no place even to lay his head,'*" where did I get the idea that I should have such a nice, comfortable life if I'm going to be treated the same way Jesus was? I straightened up and stared at the wall in amazement as I realized Jesus was trying to tell me that in HIS kingdom, I was to EXPECT hard times! He even went so far as to say He would be the cause of this trouble, "*Do not suppose that I have come to bring peace to the earth. I did not come to bring peace, but a sword. For I have come to turn 'a man against his father, a daughter against her mother, a daughter-in-law against her mother-in-law—a man's enemies will be the members of his own household.'*" (Matthew 10:34-36).

Not willing to give up my dream of a peaceful, happy life, I began to wonder if only Jesus was treated poorly. "Perhaps the disciples fared better," I comforted myself. I turned to Acts to look at the life of Peter—the head of the new church Jesus directed the disciples to start—only to find he was jailed and flogged more than once as a result of attempting to obey the Lord at all times. Peter reiterates all that Jesus said in the gospels as though we're foolish to expect anything else, "*Dear friends, don't be surprised at the fiery trials you are going through, as if something strange were happening to you.*" (1 Peter 4:12). He continues in that vein by saying, "*Dear friends, I urge you, as foreigners and exiles, to abstain from sinful desires, which wage war against your soul.*" (1 Peter 2:11). He even calls us strangers and foreigners so we remember we're not supposed to hunker down and get comfortable, or have any expectations of good times and lots of rewards. In 1 Peter 1:6-7a Peter goes so far as to say these problems we're going to face are GOOD for us (*"So be truly glad. There is wonderful joy ahead, even though you have to endure many trials for a little while. These trials will show that your faith is genuine."*). Peter adds, for good measure, that we are to always do the right thing even if it causes trouble for us (*"For God called you to do good, even if it means suffering, just as Christ suffered for you. He is your example, and you must follow in his steps."* 1 Peter 2:21).

"Okay, fine, Lord," I muttered. "Peter had a rough life, but what about Paul who wrote a good chunk of the New Testament? Surely you blessed him with a nice, comfortable life, right?" I frantically flipped pages until I came to 2 Corinthians 11:24-28 and read Paul's own words about what kind of life he experienced: *"Five different times the Jewish leaders gave me thirty-nine lashes. Three times I was beaten with rods. Once I was stoned. Three times I was shipwrecked. Once I spent a whole night and a day adrift at sea. I have traveled on many long journeys. I have faced danger from rivers and from robbers. I have faced danger from my own people, the Jews, as well as from the Gentiles. I have faced danger in the cities, in the deserts, and on the seas. And I have faced danger from men who claim to be believers but are not. I have worked hard and long, enduring many sleepless nights. I have been hungry and thirsty and have often gone without food. I have shivered in the cold, without enough clothing to keep me warm. Then, besides all this, I have the daily burden of my concern for all the churches."*

"What?" I exclaimed. "Why was Paul treated so badly even though he was such a godly man?" I continued to search until I found the answer in 2 Corinthians 4:8-10, *"We are pressed on every side by troubles, but we are not crushed. We are perplexed, but not driven to despair. We are hunted down, but never abandoned by God. We get knocked down, but we are not destroyed. Through suffering, our bodies continue to share in the death of Jesus so that the life of Jesus may also be seen in our bodies."* I realized Paul was saying that through suffering, we're sharing in Jesus' death which makes us become more like Him. Now I was getting mad! No one told me I was supposed to be "dying" all the time, or that I would be continually "pressed, perplexed, hunted down, and knocked down!" "That's not the kind of life I signed up for when I accepted the Lord as my Savior," I fumed. "I thought I would have a happy, blessed life and then spend eternity in a glorious, pain-free place called Heaven. How did I miss the truth of what life would look like as a fully devoted follower of Christ?"

I began to think about my training even as a child and how it played into my belief that I would live a comfortable, easy life as a Christian. I reflected on my childhood experiences where I was punished for wrong-doing, and praised and rewarded for obedience. That treatment continued throughout my schooling years as teachers gave out wonderful rewards for good behavior and top grades, and saved their punishments for those who didn't obey or strive to learn as quickly and thoroughly as possible. My job experiences reinforced my belief that good things happened to those who worked hard such as promotions, recognition, and the corner office. Those who shirked were given warnings, the worst jobs, and pink slips. On top of all that mind programming were the constant TV, magazine, and catalog ads brain-washing me on what I just HAD to have (everyone who's anyone has a), and my natural tendency to keep up with the "Jones." No wonder I was so ill-equipped to understand the truth about God's kingdom: Those who commit their whole lives to the Lord, who seek for Him with all their hearts, who humble themselves under His mighty hand, and who trust only the Lord and obey Him in all things, will receive persecutions, trials, and tribulations! Once again, I came face to face with the truth of this verse in Isaiah 55:8-9, "'*My thoughts are nothing like your thoughts,' says the LORD. 'And my ways are far beyond anything you could imagine. For just as the heavens are higher than the earth, so my ways are higher than your ways and my thoughts higher than your thoughts.*'" In fact, the thought process God wants us to have as Christians runs counter-intuitive to any human reasoning as shown in James 1:2-4, "*Dear brothers and sisters, when troubles come your way, consider it an opportunity for great joy. For you know that when your faith is tested, your endurance has a chance to grow. So let it grow, for when your endurance is fully developed, you will be perfect and complete, needing nothing.*"

"God," I whined. "That's just impossible to face troubles and 'consider it an opportunity for great joy!' Why would anyone sign up to become a Christian if that's all they have to look forward to? What did you say? I'm wrong? There IS something good to look forward to?" I scrambled for my Bible which had fallen to the floor while I was ruminating on my Christian life from God's perspective. Flipping through the pages frantically, I searched to find any good reason for following the Lord. Well, what do you know—I found lots of good reasons! The problem for my impatient mind is that while God DOES promise rewards and recognition, He believes in delayed-gratification! Most of the good things promised in His word happen in the future as it says in Romans 8:18, *"Yet what we suffer now is nothing compared to the glory he will reveal to us later."* James 1:12 reinforces this truth, *"God blesses those who patiently endure testing and temptation. Afterward they will receive the crown of life that God has promised to those who love him."*

Understanding began to flood my heart as I saw God's plan for His children. This life is to be a testing ground to build our character and prepare us for our real life in Heaven. We HAVE to face trials in order to be strengthened and to grow our faith (*These trials will show that your faith is genuine. It is being tested as fire tests and purifies gold—though your faith is far more precious than mere gold. So when your faith remains strong through many trials, it will bring you much praise and glory and honor on the day when Jesus Christ is revealed to the whole world."* I Peter 1:7), but God promises to be with us always (*And I will ask the Father, and he will give you another Advocate, who will never leave you."* John 14:16), and to help us in each trial (*Many are the afflictions of the righteous, but the Lord delivers him out of them all."* Psalms 34:19). The help does come, eventually, according to His perfect timing, in the way He knows is best for each of us.

I sat back on my bed amazed at how wrong I had been in my expectations of what life and God "owed" me. I began to realize that I couldn't anticipate comfort, ease, or blessings at all! Sure they might come, but only as God decided they would be good for me at a particular time in my life. The rest of the time, I needed to not only accept, but to embrace the trials and tribulations that would surely come since the Lord PROMISED them, and to realize they happen for my good. "What's my choice?" I muttered. "I can be unhappy, dissatisfied, and depressed, or

I can experience the life God promised me!" (*"I pray that God, the source of hope, will fill you completely with joy and peace because you trust in him. Then you will overflow with confident hope through the power of the Holy Spirit."* Romans 15:13). "Just think!" I exclaimed. "God's offering me peace, joy, and hope! What wonderful gifts, and yet He's not done! He's also promising me incredible rewards, and happiness in Heaven as it says in 1 Corinthians 2:9, " . . . *'No eye has seen, no ear has heard, and no mind has imagined what God has prepared for those who love him.'"*

By now I was getting excited about my new life! "Okay, God, I get it," I shouted. "I have YOU as my best friend here on earth no matter what trials I have to experience, and I have an incredible future to look forward to as the 'frosting on the cake!' Besides all that, you've promised a valuable life for me here on earth *("For I know the plans I have for you," declares the LORD, "plans to prosper you and not to harm you, plans to give you hope and a future."* Jeremiah 29:11*)*.

Slowly, I sank to my knees by my bed and made the commitment the Lord had been patiently waiting for: "Here are my expectations, Lord. I give them all to you—my need to always see and understand WHY You're doing WHAT You're doing, my desperate craving for comfort and an easy life, and my selfish longing for only blessings with no suffering ever required. I will no longer allow myself to live with a sense of entitlement, but will instead search for the joy, peace, and strength you promised me to make sure I can endure my problems." As I rose from my knees, I sensed a smile of pleasure emanating from the Lord, and real, honest-to-goodness peace filled my heart. "Hey!" I beamed. "Maybe life devoid of all expectations to have only harmony and enjoyment as my daily fare won't be so bad after all. In fact, this kind of life could actually be intoxicating! Who knows what I may become once I've experienced all the trials God has in store for me? Maybe I'll become the best version of myself that's possible and earn incredible rewards in Heaven. Wouldn't that be cool?" With joy in my heart, I set out on my day, the only expectations in my mind being the fact that troubles WOULD come, but so would the rewards and blessings, someday, somewhere down the road. Now those are expectations I can depend on!

----

1. How do you feel about the hardships and troubles in your life? Have you seen any good come of them? If so, give examples _____

_____

_____

_____

2. Do you have expectations for what your life should look like now that you've agreed to serve the Lord? If so, what are they? _____

_____

_____

_____

3. Do you think Paul, Peter, and John had any expectations for what their lives as Christ-followers would look like? If their expectations did not line up with their reality, do you think they were disappointed or shocked? Do you think their faith failed or suffered? How do you think they lined up their expectations with God's reality? _____

_____

_____

_____

4. Have you ever been tempted to hang out on the fringes of Christianity hoping you won't have to suffer like Paul, Peter, and John did? _____

_____

_____

_____

5. What do you think about the expectations of the rich young ruler who was told to give all his money to the poor and follow Jesus? HIS expectations were dashed. Speculate on how you think his life turned out after that? _____

_____

_____

_____

6. Do you think Americans are more prone to have expectations than people in other countries? Why or why not? _____

_____

_____

_____

7. What would your life look like if you had no expectations other than to have peace, joy, and hope? Explain _____

_____

_____

_____

8. What would it take for you to give up all your expectations including comfort, ease of living, blessings, happiness, and the fulfillment of all your dreams? Explain in detail as honestly as possible _____

_____

_____

_____

9. Are you willing to give up your sense of entitlement now that you know the truth of what God actually promised you? Why or why not?

_____

_____

_____

_____

Chapter 11

WHAT DID YOU SAY, LORD? I CAN'T HEAR YOU!

"God, I know you want to communicate with me, and I want to hear from you (*"My sheep listen to my voice; I know them, and they follow me."* John 10:27), but it's so hard to actually know what you're saying! How can I be sure it's **your** voice I'm sensing, or if it's only my own thoughts, or just someone else's opinion? What if it's Satan confusing me? What if I follow that "voice" and find out it's wrong? What if I end up with terrible consequences for trying to obey what I think is You? After all, many people have done horrible things in this world and said, 'God told me do it!', and people who are sick with mental illnesses are known to hear voices. I'm sorry, God, but the risk is just too great. It feels much safer to follow my own thoughts and my ability to reason my way through each situation. I haven't done too badly on my own this far . . . ."

Convinced I was better off ignoring the whole subject of God speaking to me, I attempted to move on and live life the best I knew how. The problem was that I wasn't happy! I felt like I was missing out on a vital component of friendship with the Lord. After all, who wants to just talk to a wall? What good was prayer if God couldn't respond to me like a close friend would? I kept making mistakes, and I realized I **wasn't** a good judge of how to successfully run my life. Determined to take another look at the possibility that I COULD hear God's voice clearly and accurately (after all, He IS God, and He should be able to make Himself and His desires known perfectly to me) I began to look at what God, Himself, says about the whole idea.

Well, it came as somewhat of a shock that God mostly wants to speak to me through His Word! He put much time and effort into spelling out who He is and what He wants me to do with my life, and He expects me to read this incredible guidebook often, if not every day ("*But they* [godly people] *delight in the law of the Lord, meditating on it day and night.*" Psalm 1:2*).* How did I think I could navigate through this scary, dangerous wilderness called life without constantly referring to God's map? Why was I so willing to cavalierly step into each day with only my reasoning to guide me around the land mines? Why did I think I could find the right pathway without an experienced guide? Obviously, I couldn't, or I wouldn't be searching for help! Here's what God says I need, "*Your word is a lamp to guide my feet and a light for my path.*" (Psalm 119:105). Hebrews 4:12 adds additional proof for the effectiveness of the Bible in giving me daily direction, "*For the word of God is alive and powerful. It is sharper than the sharpest two-edged sword, cutting between soul and spirit, between joint and marrow. It exposes our innermost thoughts and desires.*" I read on so amazed that I had missed the incredible value of God's Word to fill my life with joy and peace, and to help me always make the right decisions. Just listen to THIS description of the value of God's words: *The instructions of the Lord are perfect, reviving the soul. The decrees of the Lord are trustworthy, making wise the simple.*" (Psalm 19:7). I think God summed up the value of the Bible perfectly in 2 Timothy 3:16-17, "*All Scripture is inspired by God and is useful to teach us what is true and to make us realize what is wrong in our lives. It corrects us when we are wrong and teaches us to do what is right. God uses it to prepare and equip his people to do every good work.*"

"Okay, Lord," I relented. "I see now that I have to put tremendous focus and desire into reading your words in order to hear your voice. But what about the situations not covered in the Bible? What about when I need instant guidance and direction for a particular situation? What should I do then?" I didn't hear any quick answers, but I did wonder if God could just nudge me in those times so I wouldn't make a mistake. I know He doesn't want me to sin or to go in the wrong direction, but sometimes I truly don't know what to do!

Well, until I figured out this dilemma of hearing directly from the Lord, I did the safe thing and opened my Bible. Suddenly my next step in learning to discern God's will for every detail of my life became very clear as I read Romans 12:2, *"Don't copy the behavior and customs of this world, but let God transform you into a new person by changing the way you think. Then you will learn to know God's will for you, who is good and pleasing and perfect."* My problem with distinctly hearing the voice of the Lord is my contaminated thought process! I have to change the way I think, first! It stands to reason that if my thought process has been corrupted by the worldly system I'm inundated by every day, not to mention my own sinful nature, I need to have it washed clean. In great excitement I searched for words talking about being washed, and wouldn't you know it, I found Ephesians 5:25-26, *" . . . just as Christ loved the church. He gave up his life for her to make her holy and clean, washed by the cleansing of God's word."* Once again I was confronted with the value of continually reading God's Word, if for no other reason than to obtain a clean, pure heart! Just to make sure I remembered the importance of the cleansing of God's Word on my thoughts, I also "happened" onto Psalm 119:9, *"How can a young person stay pure? By obeying your word."*

Next, as I continued to search the Bible, I realized that another huge key to hearing and understanding the guidance of the Lord was the gift of the Holy Spirit I received at my spiritual birth. Here's what Jesus said about the Holy Spirit, *"But when the Father sends the Advocate as my representative—that is, the Holy Spirit—he will teach you everything and will remind you of everything I have told you."* Just think! Jesus put His own spirit in me so I have no excuse for not following Him perfectly. He's actually inhabiting my mind at all times, and, in fact, He wants to take over my whole being as Galatians 2:20 says, *"My old self has been crucified with Christ. It is no longer I who live, but Christ lives in me. So I live in this earthly body by trusting in the Son of God, who loved me and gave himself for me."* This Holy Spirit is really good about agitating me over and over when I'm going the wrong way, and sending peace and encouragement when I'm going the right way. He also promises something pretty incredible in Luke 12:11-12, *"And when you are brought to trial in the synagogues and before rulers and authorities, don't worry about how to defend yourself or what to say, for the Holy Spirit will teach you at that time what needs to be said."* There's also a verse in Matthew 10:19-20 that says, *"When you are arrested, don't worry about how to respond or what to say. God will give you the right words at the right time. For it is not you who will be speaking—it will be the Spirit of your Father speaking through you."* It sounds like if we're attempting to follow the Lord, the Holy Spirit will even help us know what to say! Added to that incredible promise is the one where He promises to PRAY for us when we don't know how to pray as Romans 8:26 says, *"And the Holy Spirit helps us in our weakness. For example, we don't know what God wants us to pray for. But the Holy Spirit prays for us with groaning's that cannot be expressed in words."* What wonderful benefits! Actually God says in 1 Corinthians 2:16, *"For, 'Who can know the LORD's thoughts? Who knows enough to teach him?' But we understand these things, for we have the mind of Christ."* How cool is that? God's very own mind is right inside of me! It's like having the Creator, the one who MADE me, available 24/7!

"Okay, Lord, I'm starting to get it," I squealed excitedly. "Hearing God's voice perfectly is a process, just like getting to know a friend! The more I read your Word and the more I listen to the Holy Spirit, the more I'll start to understand your character and desires, and to know if it's really You speaking to me. Is that it, or is there more to having sharp ears?" Once again, my continued searching of the Bible turned up more clues! I realized prayer is another critical component in my search to clearly hear the voice of the Lord. James 1:5 says, *"If you need wisdom, ask our generous God, and he will give it to you. He will not rebuke you for asking."* I saw that I have to start asking Him for help if I want Him to communicate with me and guide me. It almost sounded like in James 4:2, *" . . . you don't have what you want because you don't ask God for it,"* that it's **my fault** if I don't know God's will unless I'm asking Him for it. I also have to be willing to LISTEN for Him to speak as Psalm 37:7 directs me to do, *"Be still in the presence of the Lord, and wait patiently for him to act."* I realized that God is an all or nothing God! He doesn't want to just flit in and out of my life based on my decision of whether or not I need Him that day. Instead He says in Proverbs 3:5-6, *"Trust in the Lord with all your heart; do not depend on your own understanding. Seek his will in all* *you do, and he will show you which path to take."* I have to keep praying, keep asking about everything, and continue to be desperate for His will and direction in order for Him to guide me in choosing the right path to take. "What an incredible promise if it's really true," I murmured, wanting to believe, but wondering if God's words were really just a nice platitude. God didn't leave me hanging, though, since I quickly found the reason to actually believe Him when I read 1 Peter 5:7, *"Give all your worries and cares to God, for he cares about you."* There's the answer!" I shouted, jumping up and down with delight. "It's because He LOVES me that He's anxious to listen to my prayers and then guide my footsteps. I can trust a God like that!"

Wanting to make sure I wasn't missing any other way God might want to speak to me, I reviewed what I had so far: Immersing myself in His word, the Holy Spirit guiding my thoughts, and much time spent in prayer. "I don't want to overlook any important means You use to teach me and supply me with wisdom," I assured the Lord, so I began looking once again into His resourceful Word. To my shock and disbelief, I discovered that He often uses other people to speak truth into my life! Proverbs 11:14 says, *"Without wise leadership, a nation falls; there is safety in having many advisers."* To make matters worse, Proverbs 12:15 even calls me a fool if I don't want to listen to others, *"Fools think their own way is right, but the wise listen to others."*

"I don't like this avenue You use to speak to me, Lord," I remonstrated. "What if I don't like what they say? What if I don't like THEM? What if they're wrong? I'm okay reading the Scripture and listening to the Holy Spirit, but I don't like the idea of having to listen to others! What's that you're saying, Lord? You know I'm still hard of hearing! What did You say? You're telling me to test what they say? (*"Dear friends, do not believe everyone who claims to speak by the Spirit. You must test them to see if the spirit they have comes from God. For there are many false prophets in the world."* 1 John 4:1). "Well, how am I supposed to do that?" I grumbled. "You told me I have no wisdom on my own, and You said not to trust in my own understanding . . . . Pardon me? Oh, right, I'm supposed to use the standards in Your Word? You'll never guide me to do something contrary to your Word? Well, I guess we've come full circle, haven't we,

Lord," I sighed. "That's what Joshua 1:8 is trying to say, isn't it," I mused as I read the verse out loud, "*Study this Book of Instruction continually. Meditate on it day and night so you will be sure to obey everything written in it. Only then will you prosper and succeed in all you do.*"

"I know you speak through circumstances, as well, Lord," I said as I was wrapping up my research. "If my company goes out of business, or if my apartment that I rent is bought by someone, or if various other events out of my control happen, I understand that You're giving guidance and direction that way, also. Now that I've covered all the ways You speak to me, though, I don't understand why I have such a hard time using them. In fact, most Christians I know would say they struggle to hear your voice, too. What makes such straightforward guidelines so difficult to actually practice?" Well, God, who has such wisdom and insight into the human heart, guided me to Hebrews 3:15, "*Today when you hear his voice, don't harden your hearts as Israel did when they rebelled.*" I bowed my head in shame as I realized the truth of this verse; often I don't "hear" God's voice because I don't want to listen to what He's telling me. I came to understand that the consequences of hardening my heart by refusing to listen to the Lord was described in I Timothy 4:2, "*These people are hypocrites and liars, and their consciences are dead.*" (Some versions say "their consciences are seared as with a hot iron!"). I shuddered to think of my conscience becoming so covered with scar tissue from disobedience that I would no longer even **be able** to hear the voice of the Lord! On the spot, I made the commitment to the Lord that with His help, I would seek to have a soft and pliable heart, the consistency of warm wax and wet clay, toward His guidance. I wanted to be just like Samuel, the young boy, who responded to God's voice in Samuel 3:10, "*And the LORD came and called as before, "Samuel! Samuel!" And Samuel replied, "Speak, your servant is listening.*"

"Are there any other reasons I struggle to hear your voice clearly?" I tentatively questioned the Lord. As the answer came from 1 John 5:14-15, I read it with a sickening sensation in my stomach; "*And we are confident that he hears us whenever we ask for anything that pleases him. And since we know he hears us when we make our requests, we also know that he will give us what we ask for.*" No wonder there are times I can't hear Him," I thought. "Sometimes I'm so sure I know what's best for me and I'm demanding that He answer my request when it might not be His will for me." Slowly, it dawned on me that just like I do with my children when they pester me for something that's not good for them, the Lord turns a deaf ear to my prayers until I pray in line with His will. Stunned at that revelation of the reason for God's silence, I read this verse in Psalm 66:18 describing another reason God won't listen to my prayers, let alone respond to them; "*If I had not confessed the sin in my heart, the Lord would not have listened.*" I realized that my fear of following the Lord, and my lack of faith in His wisdom clogs my ear canals with static as does my pride in thinking I know what is best for me. As clarity filled my mind showing me that sometimes I'm a bad listener, or I'm expecting the Lord to speak when my requests are all out of kilter with His will, or I'm harboring sin in my life, I fell to my knees begging God to heal my ears so I could always hear Him well! (Mark 4:9, *"Then he said, "Anyone with ears to hear should listen and understand.").* "I want these verses to be true of me at all times," I pleaded with the Lord: "*The gatekeeper opens the gate for him* [the Good Shepherd]*, and the sheep recognize his voice and come to him. He calls his own sheep by name and leads them out. After he has gathered his own flock, he walks ahead of them, and they follow him because they know his voice.*" As I knelt before the Lord, I realized that "*Anyone with ears to hear must listen to the Spirit and understand what he is saying to the churches.*" (Revelation 3:13). A picture flashed behind my closed eyes of me running with wild, reckless, joyful abandonment to obey every word from the mouth of the Lord. I saw my face, and it was focused, determined, desperate, deliberate, and intentional to follow Him, no matter what it cost me, no matter how hard, painful, or scary it might be to obey His directives. I realized that I was actually scared to death of the consequences of NOT hearing every single prompting of the Holy Spirit, and of NOT obeying them. As the picture continued to stream through my mind's eye, I saw myself turning my head, and I could see my ears wide opened, completely free of the plugs that had rendered me so deaf to the Lord's whispers. I sensed in my spirit that the Lord was watching the picture, too, and He was delighted with His child's new hearing abilities!

----

1. Have you ever sensed the Holy Spirit prompting you to do something or to hold back? How did you respond? _____

_____

_____

_____

2. On a scale of 0-10 how difficult do you find it to discern God's voice from all the other stimuli coming your way? How often are you correct in picking out His voice? Explain _____

_____

_____

_____

3. What percentage of the time do you make decisions based on promptings from the Lord? What do you base your decisions on the rest of the time? Are you pleased with the outcome of your decisions? Why or why not? _____

_____

_____

_____

4. What is the greatest hindrance for you in hearing the voice of the Lord? Why? _____

_____

_____

_____

5. What do you think of the idea that God wants to mostly speak to you through His word? If you really believed that truth, would you spend more time reading the Bible and seeking to be open to the guidance and direction of the Holy Spirit as you read? Explain _____

_____

_____

_____

6. What percentage of the time do you fail to hear God's word because you don't WANT to hear it? On a scale of 0-10, how harmful will that attitude be to your future? Explain _____

_____

_____

_____

7. How do you feel about receiving the guidance of the Lord through other people? Has that ever happened to you? Are you open to listening to others including your children, spouse, friends, or even an enemy? Why or why not? _____

_____

_____

_____

8. Do you think God can use an enemy to teach you? If so, would you reconsider enemies as agents of God? Would that help you to forgive your enemies? Why or why not? _____

_____

_____

_____

9. What do you think of the truth that God won't even listen to you if you have sin in your heart? Does that knowledge spur you to deal with sin quicker once you become aware of it? Why or why not? _____

_____

_____

_____

10. What about the verses telling us to pray only in line with God's will, or He won't hear us? Does that truth encourage you to pray more carefully, or does it discourage you from praying as much? Explain _____

_____

_____

_____

11. On a scale of 0-10, how much do you really care if God speaks to you or not? Do you value that part of your friendship? Why or why not? Do you think your life would change for the better if you were able to clearly hear Him every time He chose to whisper to or prompt you? Explain

_____

_____

_____

_____

Chapter 12

MY DRIVING EXPERIENCES

How much influence do back-seat passengers have on the direction a car is traveling? Oh, they can be loud and obnoxious; they can lean forward and give their opinions on the path being traveled; they can beg and plead with the driver to change directions, to speed up, or to slow down; they can even threaten to jump out if the driver doesn't do things their way, but in reality, they have no effect directly on what the driver chooses to do with the control he has over the vehicle. They are forced to put themselves under the jurisdiction of the driver with no say in the decisions he makes. No wonder I fought to be the driver of my automobile! "The driver has choices," I reasoned. "The driver appears to be in control, and the driver is the most important person in the car," I concluded. There was just one problem with my desire to be the driver—I didn't have the training or the wisdom to make good choices in driving through life. I crashed my vehicle with great regularity. I was often lost. I ran out of gas frequently because I forgot to check the gauges and when the car broke down, I had no idea how to fix it so I could proceed on my journey. In spite of my poor track record, though, I hung onto the steering wheel of my car with every atom of my being.

While I soon began to understand that there was someone in the car far superior to me in all ways including successful car-driving, I wasn't willing to give up my spot. You see, the idea of being in the backseat with no say in my life was intolerable, and so I just tried harder to be a good driver. Well, the day came when the ultimate crash happened—the day when I finally realized I needed help. In desperation I invited the Lord to come and sit in the passenger's seat instead of the back seat, and I promised to make Him the "navigator" on my trip. I still had control (what a relief!), but I was paying more attention to what He said—well, most of the time. If He said to slow down, I still made sure I thought about it and agreed with His request before I obeyed. If He said to turn up ahead at the next left, I wondered why He would ask me to do something that made no sense to me, so sometimes I complied, but other times I went the way that seemed right to me. Some days I got so caught up in the journey, I even forgot He was there! Perhaps He was giving me guidance, but if He was, I never heard it.

Eventually I began to realize I wasn't having much fun in life. Sure, I was in control (or so I thought) which made me feel safe, but I had no great stories to tell of God's blessings and miracles. My journey was dull and boring, and I knew I wasn't reaching the wonderful potential I sensed was buried deep beneath my craving for comfort and ease. Finally, I'd had enough of driving! I gathered my courage and ventured the question: "Would you be willing to trade places with me?" His eyes lit up, and with great delight on His face, He opened his car door and circled around to the driver's side while I fearfully slid over. As He closed the door and put the car in gear, I began to give Him instructions on where to go and what to do on this journey. I wasn't so sure He could do a good job without my help. As you can imagine, my attempt to hang onto control didn't go over very well. He didn't LISTEN to me! I stressed out, wrung my hands over the direction we were heading, and gazed with fear and trepidation at the world outside my windshield. Suddenly, though, it dawned on me—we were having fun! Life was about others instead of me, and I found that my new focus filled me with joy and satisfaction. I saw how many crashes He avoided, and when we DID get bumped, He knew how to steer around the mess and find the way back onto the right road. I lost my fear! I became strong in my complete trust of this new driver and excited about the pathway we were traveling along. I'm sure you've guessed what happened next—I crawled into the "hated" backseat, content to enjoy the scenery, free to communicate with my Perfect Driver, and to wait with great anticipation to see where this new road would lead us.

These days, whenever I'm tempted to crawl back into the front seat or even grab hold of the steering wheel, I remember the stress of being in charge of my life; the crashes, the fear, and the loneliness of trying to navigate my car safely through the potholes of life. I quickly settle back into my wonderful place in the backseat, content to bask in the peace of **not** being in control, and the joy of knowing my Driver has everything covered. What an incredible way to live my life, and how completely I'm coming to understand the benefits of having a chauffeur!

----

1. What's your most comfortable position in the car? Why? _____

_____

_____

_____

2. Where do you spend most of your time in the car? Have you ever moved your position? If so, how did that make you feel? _____

_____

_____

_____

3. Have you ever experienced a "crash" in life? Did it cause you to rethink your position in the car? Why or why not? _____

_____

_____

_____

4. Describe in detail what your life would look like if the Lord were driving. How do you feel about that description? Is it attractive to you? Why or why not? _____

_____

_____

_____

5. Do you trust God to exclusively drive your car? Why or why not?

_____

_____

_____

_____

6. What would it take for you to ever let the Lord be in charge of your life all the time with no say on your part (i.e. you become a backseat passenger)? Explain _____

_____

_____

_____

Chapter 13

MY STRUGGLES THIS WEEK

For some reason when I became a Christian, I didn't understand the truth that I had the choice of two pathways to travel along in my spiritual journey. So I, like many other new Christians who are also oblivious to this critical piece of information, chose the pathway called "Following my Own Agenda." After praying for God's support, I began attempting to follow the Lord the best way I knew how. I memorized scripture, became very familiar with the Bible and its teachings, served in my gifted areas, watched other Christians for clues on how to be successful, and used my valuable thought process to plan out my daily life and assess how I was doing on my journey. After many bumps and bruises along the way, however, I desperately began reaching out to the Lord more for help and strength. Eventually, I came to understand that there was another pathway available to me, and it was called "Following Only God's Agenda." This pathway seemed to be calling out to me, and I did what most Christians do at this point in their spiritual growth. I put one foot on each pathway and tried to straddle my way through life—doing enough of God's agenda to keep the guilt away, but following my own agenda when it made more sense, or when I felt the circumstances warranted me taking control. Of course, this "fence-sitting" didn't bring me the peace I was craving, nor did it give me the guidance and direction I knew I needed.

One day, in a moment of courage (and desperation), I took my foot off the "Following my Own Agenda" pathway, and planted both feet in the pathway called, "Following Only God's agenda." Much to my amazement and excitement, I found that this pathway was strewn with peace, joy, contentment, and such gratitude I could hardly grasp it all. I found great opportunities to serve the Lord that brought wonderful results for kingdom purposes. I saw miracles happen like I'd never seen before. I felt my love for the Lord growing by leaps and bounds, and I saw evidence of Him all along the way. The Bible came alive right before my eyes, and I began to gain wisdom that was elusive before. I never wanted to go back to the other pathway, well at least, not until this week. You see, on this new pathway, I have to walk by faith, not by sight. I have to keep my hands off every situation and not open my mouth unless the Lord tells me I can. Only after I stepped onto this pathway, did I realize I'd given up my right to have ANY say in ANY thing! I have to keep all avenues open for Him to speak to me (even through my kids and my enemies!), and then I have to obey every time, no matter how I feel about what He's asking me to do or to say—"What if they don't understand? What if they turn on me? What if I'm laughed at? What if I'm hung out to dry? What if, just this one time, I misunderstood God's voice?" I can no longer default to my old comfortable ways that I know by heart. I can't hide or by-pass troubling situations. I can't use my thought process to figure things out AT ALL, nor can I jump in and do what seems to me to be the right thing to do.

The problem is that on THIS pathway, God rules supreme, and He doesn't need or WANT my thoughts on a situation—after all, His ways are HIGHER than my ways and He doesn't use common sense or logic to guide me. He actually asks me to jump off cliffs without a safety harness and just trust that underneath are the everlasting arms. When I complain that I don't understand what He's up to, or that He's working too slowly, He just says things like, "Rest in the Lord. Wait patiently for Him to work." Then He asks me to go into situations or act in ways that make no sense to me, let alone to the people around me. Well, that's another story altogether—you know, how people view me. Before, when I was walking the "Following My Own Agenda" pathway, I could do image-management, I could pick and choose what I was going to say or do, I could be a people-pleaser to my heart's content, and I could blame others if things didn't work out so well. Not so on this pathway! As I looked with longing at that other pathway, I suddenly remembered the blessings, the miracles, the intense, perfect, daily love of my Heavenly Father, and my glorious future awaiting up ahead where I'm laying up treasures, and then I remembered that these "perks" are only available on the pathway called "Following Only God's Agenda." Suddenly it didn't matter how I was scorned, or reproved, or looked down on, or ignored, or passed over for friendships and opportunities. All that mattered was the shine of God's face on me, and the gentle hug I felt in my soul. I pulled my tattered heart together, put my hand in God's big, safe hand and, never looking back, firmly walked with His courage and strength along the pathway He chose for me.

----

1. Were you aware when you became a Christian that there were two pathways to choose from? Explain _____

_____

_____

_____

2. Which pathway did you choose when you gave your heart to the Lord? Why? _____

_____

_____

_____

3. How did your choice of a pathway negatively or positively impact your outcomes in life? Explain _____

_____

_____

_____

4. Can you relate to the idea of having one foot on each pathway, and trying to straddle the two opposing avenues? If so, give some examples

_____

_____

_____

_____

5. If you are not solely walking on the "Following Only God's Agenda" pathway, what would it take for you to choose that option? Explain

_____

_____

_____

_____

6. If you've chosen to walk the "Following Only God's Agenda" pathway, describe what it's been like. What do you like about it? What parts do you find difficult? Have you ever wanted to change your mind and go back to the other pathway? Explain _____

_____

_____

_____

7. How do you handle the trials and tribulations that come on that pathway? Give some examples _____

_____

_____

_____

Chapter 14

HELP—MY ARMOR HAS GAPS!

I know God has provided me with armor so I don't get wounded or taken out in this spiritual battle I'm embroiled in, but why am I struggling so much to put the armor on and KEEP it on? God commands me to put it on, but I can't find the instructions! Maybe there's a clue in these verses in Ephesians 6:10-18:

"Be strong in the Lord and in his mighty power. Put on all of God's armor so that you will be able to stand firm against all strategies of the devil. For we are not fighting against flesh-and-blood enemies, but against evil rulers and authorities of the unseen world, against mighty powers in this dark world, and against evil spirits in the heavenly places.

Therefore, put on every piece of God's armor so you will be able to resist the enemy in the time of evil. Then after the battle you will still be standing firm. Stand your ground, putting on the belt of truth and the body armor of God's righteousness. For shoes, put on the peace that comes from the Good News so that you will be fully prepared. In addition to all of these, hold up the shield of faith to stop the fiery arrows of the devil. Put on salvation as your helmet, and take the sword of the Spirit, which is the word of God.

Pray in the Spirit at all times and on every occasion. Stay alert and be persistent in your prayers for all believers everywhere."

Okay, so it's obvious that I have to put on every bit of this armor and make sure it's in working order at all times in order to win my fight against Satan and his millions of henchmen. The Bible says, *"Stay alert! Watch out for your great enemy, the devil. He prowls around like a roaring lion, looking for someone to devour."* (1 Peter 5:8). It's becoming clear to me that the danger is real, and I need to don this armor as quickly as possible since it appears to be the only way to be strong, powerful, and a winner in life's daily conflicts.

The first piece of armor mentioned in these verses is the belt of truth. I know the Bible contains the truth about God and His wonderful gift of Salvation—I wonder if that's how I tightly cinch my belt? Maybe I have to gain greater knowledge than I presently have in order to keep this belt from falling off. Suddenly, a thought comes to me! What about this verse in John 8:32 that says, *"And you will know the truth, and the truth will set you free?"* What if, besides knowing the truth about God so I'm not tripped up by false doctrine, I also need to know the truth about myself so I can be free of the lies Satan whispers to me? What if I choose to be so transparent with the Lord, others, and myself, that Satan can't attack me by using deception against me, or lure me into the tangles of denial? I get it! As long as I seek the truth about God, and stay open and humble toward the truth about myself, my belt appears to lock onto me for good.

The next piece of armor is the body suit of righteousness. I don't know about you, but I sure want my whole body protected in this fight! How do I get myself into this armor though, and then keep it in place? Some days I feel like my body is covered only in tatters of metal that allow lots of arrows to come right into my inner being and knock me down. The dictionary defines righteousness as "characterized by, proceeding from, or in accordance with accepted standards of morality, justice, or uprightness." That's it! I found a clue! I'm to live according to the standards God set for me in the Bible. If I don't follow His guidelines, I allow my armor to become torn, or even worse, to actually fall off. Sure enough, here's what the Bible has to say about being righteous, *"If you fully obey the Lord your God and carefully keep all his commands that I am giving you today, the Lord your God will set you high above all the nations of the world. You will experience all these blessings if you obey the Lord your God."* Deuteronomy 28:1-2. As unacceptable as it is in this day and age to seek God's righteousness, and as foolish as others think I look when I follow all of God's commands, it's worth it to me to still be standing strong after yet another attack from Satan.

Next the Bible talks about the need for shoes of peace coming from the Good News. I would think shoes are the least important part of the suit of armor, but have you ever tried to run or even walk outside with no shoes on? When my feet are bruised, scratched, and bleeding, it's pretty hard to be effective in a battle! How do I find peace, and how do I keep those "peaceful" shoes from wearing out? Some days I even forget to put them on because I ignore how wonderful the Good News of Jesus Christ really IS! Well, as usual, the Bible has the answer in Philippians 4:6-7, *"Don't worry about anything; instead, pray about everything. Tell God what you need, and thank him for all he has done. Then you will experience God's peace, which exceeds anything we can understand. His peace will guard your hearts and minds as you live in Christ Jesus."* Aha! So worry is the culprit! No wonder my shoes aren't fitting so well these days. If I just turn my worrying into praying, God will pour His peace into me so I can be about the business of bringing His kingdom down here to earth, AND my feet will be protected!

The shield of faith is next on the list. Okay, so I have a hard time with my shield. It's heavy and awkward, and most of the time, I leave it lying on the ground. No wonder I feel run through so many times, and that I spend more time in a heap in the mud than I do standing firm. What IS faith anyway? This verse popped into my mind, and I stopped to think about it. Hebrews 11:1 says, *"Faith is the confidence that what we hope for will actually happen; it gives us assurance about things we cannot see."* So these words mean I just have to keep trusting God's promises! If He promised it, it will happen. Now that I know how important this shield is to protect me, I wonder how I GET this shield of faith and how I will have the strength to carry it in a ready position at all times. In shock I read this verse, *"These trials will show that your faith is genuine. It is being tested as fire tests and purifies gold—though your faith is far more precious than mere gold. So when your faith remains strong through many trials, it will bring you much praise and glory and honor on the day when Jesus Christ is revealed to the whole world."* 1 Peter 1:7. Another clue! If I'm understanding this verse correctly, it's telling me that all the trials I go through are automatically forming and strengthening my shield. All I have to do is let the Lord have His way when the trials hit, and I'll have the best shield on the block!

Next these verses list the helmet of Salvation. While I desperately want my head protected, my helmet isn't very comfortable. It bounces around and doesn't fit well, plus it makes me hot and sweaty so I often leave it dangling by my chin strap. I wonder why I do that when I could so easily get wounded in such a critical area. My mind quickly produced the answer to that question, and it's found in Luke 9:26, "*If anyone is ashamed of me and my message, the Son of Man will be ashamed of that person when he returns in his glory and in the glory of the Father and the holy angels.*" Ashamed—what an ugly word, and to think I actually feel that way about my Lord. Sometimes I don't WANT people to know I'm a Christian because they might laugh at me. Sometimes I keep my commitment to Him hidden so I can act however I want at any given moment. Sometimes it just stops the questions if I don't let on that I know the Lord intimately.

Perhaps my helmet isn't so bad after all if it means that the Lord will be proud of me. Maybe I can put up with sweat and discomfort if it means my head will be protected from those fiery darts shot at me by Satan. Maybe the Lord's "well done" is a greater prize than the accolades of people around me.

And last, but certainly not least, these verses talk about the sword of the spirit. While I'm excited to finally have a weapon to fight back with, I'm not so good at sword fighting. Why couldn't my weapon be something fun like a laser beam, or an AK-47? Instead I'm stuck with this weighty, awkward sword that I can't seem to use to land any blows of substance. Wait, there's more to that verse—it says, " . . . the sword of the Spirit which is the word of God." What does THAT mean? Do I use the Bible to hit Satan? Wait! Isn't there a verse about the Bible being like a sword? Sure enough, Hebrews 4:12 says, "*For the word of God is alive and powerful. It is sharper than the sharpest two-edged sword, cutting between soul and spirit, between joint and marrow. It exposes our innermost thoughts and desires.*" Okay, I think I understand. God's word is able to be used as a sword to fight back against the Devil, but how do I use it that way? Psalms 119:11 says, "*I have hidden your word in my heart that I might not sin against you.*" Oh, great! Does that mean I have to actually memorize verses so I have them ready no matter where my Bible might

be at the moment the attack occurs? I'm not good at memorizing, plus I'm too busy to make time for "hiding" effective verses in my heart. On the other hand, wouldn't I rather spend the time memorizing scripture than lying on my back in a pit where Satan's arrow felled me? Well, maybe I can post index cards around my house or take them with me in the car. What if I practiced them while I was cleaning the house or putting on my make-up? Actually, maybe I'm not such a bad sword fighter after all.

Wait, there's one more verse I just noticed in the part about the armor. It says, *Pray in the Spirit at all times and on every occasion. Stay alert and be persistent in your prayers for all believers everywhere.*" I have the feeling that prayer is like the oil for my armor. It keeps the armor in good working condition and makes it look shiny and new. As I pray persistently, I sense the Lord prompting me to notice certain areas of my armor that may need attention. He wants to make sure that when each battle is over, "I will still be standing firm." Okay, this topic of armor is starting to make a whole lot more sense to me now. I'm just glad I have a great Commander-in-Chief to keep an eye on me and help me remember what to do next! Hey, I just caught a glimpse of myself in the mirror and I think I look pretty invincible. I hope Satan thinks so, too.

----

1. In the past, how important did you think the subject of spiritual armor was? How about now? Explain _____

_____

_____

_____

2. On a scale of 0-10, how diligent are you in keeping your armor on at all times? How often do you check it? Explain _____

_____

_____

_____

3. Which piece of armor is the hardest for you to keep on and in good working condition? Why? _____

_____

_____

_____

4. Do you sense when you're under spiritual attack? Why or why not?

_____

_____

_____

_____

5. Describe a time recently when you were actually still standing after a battle? What was the reason for your victory? How did it make you feel? Explain _____

_____

_____

_____

6. How hard would it be for you to actually memorize scripture? Do you think the effort is worth it? Has scripture helped you win battles in the past? Explain _____

_____

_____

_____

7. Would you pray more often, more intensely, and more specifically if you really believed prayer was a key to winning spiritual battles? Why or why not? What keeps you from praying that way? _____

_____

_____

_____

8. What does God mean when He says to "stay alert?" On a scale of 0-10, how would you rate your "alertness" quotient? Why? What would have to change in your life to make you become more alert? Explain _____

_____

_____

_____

Chapter 15

FALSE GODS IN MY LIFE?

"You must not have any other god but me" (Exodus 20:3), whispered the voice of the Lord to me one night. "I know that Lord, and I would never be so ridiculous as to build a god out of some sort of metal or wood," I replied pompously as I struggled to wake up. God ignored my sharp words and continued on, *"Do not worship any other god, for the LORD, whose name is Jealous, is a jealous God."* (Exodus 34:14). Again I declared with great confidence, "Lord, I worship only you! Look, there are no other gods in my life, not even those "gods" the church talks about like money, possessions, fame, or power. Surely the Lord will be satisfied with me now," I thought, "and I'll be able to go back to sleep." But no, once more that still small voice came to me, *"Again and again I sent all my servants the prophets to you. They said, 'Each of you must turn from your wicked ways and reform your actions; do not follow other gods to serve them. Then you will live in the land I have given to you and your fathers.' But you have not paid attention or listened to me."* (Jeremiah 35:15). By this point I was beginning to understand that the Lord was not going to leave me alone until I understood what He was saying to me, so I sat up and gave Him my full attention. But, wouldn't you know it? No more words from the Lord came into my thoughts!

By now I was fully awake and more than a little troubled by these intrusions into my plans for a good night's rest. After all, I had a big day ahead of me tomorrow and needed my wits about me. I wrapped a quilt around me and padded softly to the living room where I made a little nest on the couch. As I sat there thinking about the verses still resonating through my brain, I began to wonder what God's definition of "other" gods would sound like. Obviously, if the Bible is still relevant in this day and age, there must be more to that term than building idols out of silver or gold. I know the church teaches that we can still make things around us be our gods, but I'm sure that's not true of me. I tithe faithfully and give extra whenever the Lord prompts me. I don't have that many possessions and I'm willing to share them with others or even give them away if He asks that of me. I don't have any fame or power to speak of, nor am I in a position to gain them in the future. While I love my family dearly, I don't think I've made a god out of them. What could the Lord be referring to in His wake-up call to my spirit? Is there anyone or anything I could be tempted to worship besides Him?

Hoping I could put these upsetting thoughts out of my head and go back to sleep, I snuggled down into the quilt and closed my eyes. No such luck! Instead, various scenes began to play through my head. I pictured the Israelites going to all the trouble of creating idols, including carving out eyes, ears, mouths, and noses for them, and then setting them up in their homes and spending time worshiping them instead of the true God. "Why would they do that?" I pondered. "They had to know that the metal or clay wasn't real! How could they fake themselves out so well that they actually believed these chunks of wood had a brain, let alone the power to answer their prayers?" Little by little, I began to understand that they made idols to worship because they didn't LIKE the real God. He asked things of them that they didn't want to do. He required them to change and they didn't like that idea—change was hard, uncomfortable, awkward, and painful. He asked them to give up control of their lives and do whatever He asked them to do instead of doing whatever THEY felt like doing. They HATED His ideas and plans. They resented His interference in their lives. They disliked the rules and regulations (laws) He set in place. They couldn't see that He loved them so much He was trying to protect them and give them the best life possible. They only saw His absolutes, His commands, and His firmness, so they began to search for a way around Him. In essence, they were saying, "Hello, is anyone else up there?"

Suddenly, the scenes in my mind shifted, and I began to see myself in the place of the Israelites. I was dressed differently, of course, and the scenery was **my** home and **my** surroundings, but I saw the same feelings in my own heart that I saw in theirs. I realized that I was just as rebellious as they were even though I had judged them so harshly. While I hadn't built an idol out of metal, clay, stone, or wood, I **had** built an image in my heart of the kind of god I wanted to worship. MY god was okay with me running my own life. MY god gave me lots of leeway to have faults and shortcomings, and to blame others for them. MY god would say things like, "It's okay. No one is perfect." or, "Don't take your spiritual walk so seriously. Just relax and have a good time. It will all work out in the end, and besides, God wants you to be happy." MY god allowed me to feel superior to all those people who were obviously beneath me, and HE didn't say **anything** when I was consumed with meeting my own needs. MY god let me pick whatever path I wanted to travel each day and spent his time trying to make my life comfortable and easy. MY god was there to serve ME! I gasped in shock as I saw what I had done. MY god was not the REAL god—he was just a figment of my own thought process which was steeped in the desire to control the outcome of my life. MY god wasn't even real, let alone possessing any of the critical traits of love, strength, power, wisdom, and patience that the true God is supposed to have. I had been serving A FALSE GOD!!

By this point tears were running down my cheeks, and my quilt and I were on the floor in front of the couch as I knelt before the REAL God. I poured out my shame and my remorse for by-passing the glorious Lord and Savior, just so I could exercise the dubious right to create my own god—a god I was sure would bring me far more benefits than the God of the Bible. Because of my fear, selfishness, and lack of trust in a God who would give His life for me, I tried to take the easy way out. I somehow thought my own human, sinful, finite thought process could conjure up a better god than the real one. How wrong I was! No wonder my loving Heavenly Father—yes, the one who I was cavalierly dismissing—was concerned about the state of my heart.

As my tears continued to pour out, and my head sank farther and farther into the couch, I came to a crossroads in my heart. I could continue to take the path of least resistance and follow my own thought process, clinging to my way of doing things with a white-knuckled grip, or I could choose to trust the Lord every second of every step of every day in every situation. I had no idea this choice would be so hard, or that Satan would battle me with such a ferocious intensity throwing every fear and doubt at me that he could. Finally, as light began to filter through my living room curtains, the Lord won, and I turned my hands, palms upward, to the **only** real God. I heard Him whisper with such love and gentleness, *"Humble yourselves under the mighty power of God, and at the right time he will lift you up in honor."* (1 Peter 5:6), and so I did!

I'd like to say, "And she lived happily ever after," but the truth is that Satan continued to try and trip me up as I sought to follow only the guidance and direction of the Holy Spirit. My pathway didn't magically become easier nor did I immediately understand all the promptings of the Lord. Many times His ways made no sense to me at all, and I was strongly tempted to turn back to my false god. Other Christians around me laughed at me, called me mentally unstable, tried to reason with me that "the Lord doesn't say things like that or work like that," and even set up "interventions out of love" as they tried to persuade me that I was on the wrong track. On top of it all, my own mind was screaming at me that I was being foolish, that I was in danger, and that I would end up being a failure. "Better play it safe," I would think with relief.

Just as I was ready to throw in the towel on this new relationship with the REAL God, I would sense His incredible peace (*"I am leaving you with a gift—peace of mind and heart. And the peace I give is a gift the world cannot give. So don't be troubled or afraid."* John 14:27), and I could find the strength to go on again. At other times His love would catch me at the most unexpected times and melt my resistance into a puddle at His feet (*"How precious is your unfailing love, O God! All humanity finds shelter in the shadow of your wings."* Psalms 36:7). His wisdom showed up in such surprising ways, and it was so perfect that it satisfied the deepest parts of my heart. Okay, so maybe this real God is worth the effort it takes to follow Him even though He's so counter-intuitive. He insists that I run all guidance and direction from other people past HIM. Only HE gets to say what I keep and what I discard. He's immovable in the area of expecting me to ask HIS perspective on what I read in the Bible regardless of what the pastor says, or how I've been taught in the past, or what I think it says. He requires me to do nothing (*"Rest in the Lord; wait patiently for Him to work."* Psalms 37:7), until He says to. On the other hand, when He tells me to do something or say something, I have no choice regardless of what I think or feel about His directives. In spite of the struggles, though, this real God rewards with benefits that are out of this world! His ways really work! His blessings are fabulous! His guidance and direction are always right on, and He's completely trustworthy. I get to have a front row seat for miracles I only dreamed of in the past, and He blesses me with insights, wisdom, and abilities I am not normally capable of producing. These days, I would never go back to my false god because the real One is a thousand times better, safer, wiser, more loving, kind, and powerful. These days I can only pour out praise to the God who loved me enough to wake me up in the night and show me the truth about who I was actually worshipping!

----

1. Do you worship any of the "gods" the church talks about (money, fame, possessions, hobbies, people, music, prestige, etc.)? Why? Do you let God and your friends hold you accountable in this area so you can be sure? Why or why not? _____

_____

_____

_____

2. Can you relate to the Israelites who worshipped false gods because they didn't like the real one? How do you feel about worshipping and obeying only God, all the time? Be specific and honest. _____

_____

_____

_____

3. Do you think you've been guilty of creating a false god to worship in your heart? If so, how? How would God answer that question for you?

_____

_____

_____

_____

4. What kinds of feelings and emotions might lead someone to create a false god to worship? _____

_____

_____

_____

5. Describe in great detail the God you are currently worshipping (not who you want or wish to worship) and then share your description with a godly friend. Does it match up to the God described in the Bible? If so, how?

_____

_____

_____

_____

6. How difficult would it be to follow only God at all times? Explain. Have you ever been "shot down" for attempting to follow God? If so, how did you handle it? _____

_____

_____

_____

7. Describe a time when you knew you were completely following the Lord. What were the blessings you reaped? Did it make you want to follow Him more often or did it feel too hard? Explain _____

_____

_____

_____

8. After recognizing and submitting to the Real God, could you see yourself being tempted to create another false god? What kind of circumstances or thought processes would produce that action?

_____

_____

_____

_____

Chapter 16

THE SECRET ROOM INSIDE OF ME

"Where did that thought come from?" I wondered in dismay. "What made me act that way?" I questioned worriedly. "How could I have said those words?" I cried in a distressed voice. "I'm smarter than that, and I knew what was expected of me. What was **wrong** with me? Maybe I was just having a bad day," I consoled myself. Deep inside, though, I knew better. Something was out of kilter or even broken inside of me and I couldn't find the problem so I could fix it! I couldn't even explain it to myself let alone bring it to someone's attention who might be able to help me.

As I prayed in desperation for insight, I began to understand that I have three "rooms" inside of me. The first room I decided to call the front room. This is the area where I spend most of my time. It's the area where I interact with others, where I'm aware of all the external stimulation around me, and where I'm in control of my response to my environment. The second room I named my back room. It's where I retreat to think, ponder, process, make weighty decisions, or just hide out and chill. I'm not as aware of my surroundings in this room, and I have to be called back to the front room when someone wants my attention. I vaguely knew about these two rooms, although it helped me understand their roles in my daily life once I gave them names and descriptions. They are benign rooms that play an important part in how I handle myself throughout my day.

The third room, though, is an area that I was totally unaware of possessing. It's actually the control center of my thoughts and it functions mostly through the avenue of my subconscious mind. In that room lives a "strongman." I realized that all humans, myself included, have a strongman residing in the deepest part of our beings (The strongman is some sort of specific sin as referenced in Hebrews 12:1, " . . . *let us strip off every weight that slows us down, especially the sin that so easily trips us up . . . .*"). This strongman guides and influences everything we say and do; sometimes we're aware of this influence, but mostly it happens subconsciously.

One prevalent strongman is a lazy mind, defined as *only doing what **we** want to do **when** we want to do it*, and stubbornness is the door-keeper to that area of our lives. Stubbornness keeps us from identifying and dealing with the strongman of a lazy mind, and so, day by day, this poison becomes a greater and more powerful influence in our lives. We live with the incessant desire to have life be comfortable, easy, and pain-free. Sadly, the greatest by-product of this strongman's influence in our lives is an aura of selfishness that permeates everything we say, think, and do. We subconsciously believe that our ways are best (we develop a love-affair with our thought processes), our needs are paramount, and our desires are worthy of fulfillment and of taking precedence over the needs of anyone else or even the commands of God.

Another popular strongman is a pleasure-seeking, sensual (satisfying all of the senses) form of self-indulgence ("indulging one's own desires, passions, whims, etc., especially without restraint"), and this sin's doorkeeper is a two-headed villain combining rationalization and justification. We use these thought processes to keep us from seeing into this secret room and identifying that particular strongman. Instead we blindly continue on our merry way while the strongman worms his way into our every thought and action. We live with a narcissistic focus on seeking excitement and stimulation, and with the need to have every desire and craving fully satisfied. The by-product of this strongman is also a completely selfish focus on our own thoughts and feelings at the expense of everyone around us. We **use** people, we try to **control** people, and we **devalue** people, sacrificing others and our own spiritual well-being on the altar of self-gratification.

What's so sad is we don't comprehend that God wants to reduce our strongman to a weakling, thus bringing him to his knees. There's no other way for God to have control of a person's life ("*For who is powerful enough to enter the house of a strong man like Satan and plunder his goods? Only someone even stronger—someone who could tie him up and then plunder his house.*" Matthew 18:29). We also don't understand that with God as our partner, we become a formidable force and together can easily defeat the strongman in us. We just have to ask God to give us strength to resist the temptation to give in to our lazy mind, or our bent toward selfishness ("*For I can do everything through Christ, who gives me strength.*" Philippians 4:13).

We try in our own strength to be a better person, but we are distressfully unaware of how powerful Satan is to hang onto the footholds he's gained in our lives. The strongman doesn't like being restricted in his desires, and will fight harder, with greater tenacity, and more stealthiness to have his own way. We begin to realize that if we ever switched to the same side as God, we would actually be fighting against our own desires, and we can't bring ourselves to do such a scary, uncomfortable thing. "What if God doesn't come through for me?" we worry. "What if it hurts too much to change? What if I lose everything I care about?" We don't believe God's word where it says, "*We use God's mighty weapons, not worldly weapons, to knock down the strongholds of human reasoning and to destroy false arguments.*" (2 Corinthians 10:4). We also don't believe that God can and will help us survive that process, and that we'd be so much happier without the strongman running and ruining our lives. ("*Each time He (The Lord) said, 'My grace is all you need. My power works best in weakness.' So now I am glad to boast about my weaknesses, so that the power of Christ can work through me.*" 2 Corinthians 12:9).

As I thought about this new knowledge God had revealed to me, I bowed my head in relief, although my heart was filled with much trepidation, and signed over control of my life to the only One who knows how to overcome strongmen. In eager expectation I watched as He showed me how to starve my personal strongman ("*Submit yourselves, then, to God. Resist the devil, and he will flee from you.*" James 4:7). Much to my amazement, good things, God-honoring thoughts and actions, began to pour from my mouth and my heart. No longer did I cringe when I spoke or acted without thinking. My default mode was coming straight from the guidance of the Holy Spirit instead of from a resident, evil influence deep in my heart. Who knew that God wanted and needed to change me from the inside out, all the way deep down in that secret room?!

----

1. Were you aware of the first two rooms in your life that help you manage your thoughts? Did the description help you see when you spend time in each room? Was that image helpful to you? If so, explain _____

_____

_____

_____

2. Were you aware of the third room? Is its presence helpful to you in understanding why you act and talk as you do in spite of your best intentions? If so, give an example _____

_____

_____

_____

3. What do you think is the name of your strongman? Is he powerful or weak? Explain _____

_____

_____

_____

4. What steps are you taking to reduce the size and impact of your strongman? Give examples _____

_____

_____

_____

5. Every few weeks on a scale of 0-10, rate the size of your strongman. Do you see progress? Why or why not? _____

_____

_____

_____

6. What do you envision your life looking like without the control of the strongman? Explain in detail. Is that picture enough to keep you fighting to reduce his size no matter how hard that battle may be? Why or why not?

_____

_____

_____

_____

7. Now envision your strongman having complete control. What would that look like? _____

_____

_____

_____

8. Do you think your strongman **does** have complete control or could gain that kind of control in the future? If so, explain what could stop that scenario from happening _____

_____

_____

_____

Chapter 17

THE DOWNSIDE OF MY SPIRITUAL GIFTS

I've never felt so loved by the Lord as I did the day I discovered that He had bestowed a spiritual gift on me—actually three! It blew me away to think of His great love in crafting every part of my talents, abilities, personality, and experiences so perfectly and then, as a crowning touch, adding spiritual gifts that fit me just right. These gifts would be the main avenue He would use to help me share in bringing His will down here on earth as it is in Heaven. He would use me, through my gifts, to build up the body of Christ, and then bless me with unspeakable joy as I watched lives being reborn under the touch of the Master. What incredible goodness in the heart of God to think of such a wonderful idea—spiritual gifts!

The problem with these gifts, though, is that they only work when bathed in the wisdom and control of the Holy Spirit. We can never use them effectively apart from His guidance. If we do, and we often try to, we find out that each gift has a downside. The gift of leadership can easily morph into its owner becoming a dictator or a control freak (we've all seen them!). The gift of shepherding can create the desire to influence people in ways that God never planned for them to follow (Does pushiness ring a bell?). The gift of "helps" can cause us to take on far more responsibilities than God ever intended us to, leading us to become worn out, exhausted, and unable to find joy in our service (not knowing how, or being afraid, to just say "No"). The gift of mercy can become nothing more than an "enabling spirit" (the "pushover" when strength is needed!) The gift of creative craftsmanship can lead to great

117

pride calling attention to the artist rather than the Creator. Whether it's music, art, or acting, this gift is so tempting to turn into self-serving praise instead of exalting the Lord (ever see someone get in the way of the Lord being uplifted?) The gift of giving can demoralize the recipients if done wrongly, or it can lead to the need for attention and praise from others (How do you feel about a show-off?) The gift of teaching can lead to a focus on loving knowledge for itself, causing us to become prideful of our knowledge instead of focusing on what people need to grow spiritually (the "puffed-up" attitude?). When we use that gift according to the direction of the Holy Spirit, it causes us to have a desire to mine the depths of Scriptures to find those nuggets for hungry souls. The gift of wisdom can manifest itself in a "know-it-all" attitude, pushing everyone away from the message we are so desperately trying to communicate ("ix-nay" on the person who always knows best!). The gift of discernment can foster an angry, bitter, defeated attitude as we focus on the unfairness of life (Why can't everyone else see what I'm seeing, and why isn't anyone fixing the problem?). The gift of exhortation, also described as encouragement, can degenerate into a negative means of scolding people, thus having the effect of being a bully (I don't need another parent!). God desires that gift to always be used in a positive way to encourage and motivate people to long for a closer relationship with the Lord. The gift of administration can lead to the emphasis on tasks to the neglect and detriment of people around us (ever feel side-lined by a task??). Whenever we shut down people and their needs, or their input, or the use of THEIR gifts in order to focus on perceived time constraints, or the completion of a list, or to promote tasks at all costs, we are using that incredible gift in a way God never intended it to be used.

I realized we inflict tremendous damage to the emotions of those around us and to their desires to completely follow the Lord when we abuse these wonderful gifts. We often cover up the abusing of our precious spiritual gifts by justifying our wrong behaviors and words, and blame other people if they don't respond the way we think they should. We also avoid using our spiritual gifts at times if we don't see their value or worth, or if we think we might receive flak for using them. Sometimes we even go so far as to try and practice another spiritual gift, rationalizing that this gift is more spiritual, or perhaps it will gain us greater attention, than the ones God has given us. The saddest part about not using our gifts according the guidance of the Holy Spirit is that these gifts were meant to produce treasure in Heaven for our "real" life. When we use them incorrectly, we forfeit all rewards associated with those particular gifts. In essence, we are doing all that work for nothing! You see, a spiritual gift can be likened to receiving a beautiful wristwatch for Christmas. The watch is gorgeous, encrusted with diamonds, covered with 14-carat gold, and sporting a mother-of pearl face on the watch. The problem is that there are no batteries included, and so the watch is virtually worthless (it IS correct every 12 hours . . . .) unless we purchase batteries. The same is true of our spiritual gifts – until we receive the "batteries" required for elemental function, the gifts do us no good. The batteries for our spiritual gifts come in the form of power and direction from the Holy Spirit, and the only way to "purchase" these batteries is to fall on our knees with a humble heart and ask for them.

How we must offend and sadden the heart of the perfect Gift-giver when we don't embrace and consistently use the gifts He's given us. We hurt Him, too, when we don't ask for His guidance and direction for the perfect way to use the gifts He's entrusted into our care. May God help us to be grateful gift recipients and then masters at using them according to His will.

----

1. What do you think is your top spiritual gift? Has that been verified by people around you? If so, how often? Why is verification by others important? _____

_____

_____

_____

2. Oftentimes people have one or two additional support-type spiritual gifts that help them carry out God's will for their first gift (ex: a person with the gift of giving may also have the gift of mercy, or the person with the gift of shepherding may also have the gift of wisdom). What do you think are your second, and possibly third, spiritual gifts? Have they been verified by people around you? Explain _____

_____

_____

_____

3. Were you surprised to find out there could be a downside to your spiritual gifts? Have you ever seen a downside to your own spiritual gifts or to others around you? Give an example _____

_____

_____

_____

4. What do you think it means to use your spiritual gifts under the control of the Holy Spirit? Why do you think they don't work very well when we just decide to use them as we see fit (ex: I have the gift of giving, I see a person in need, so I decide to help them out)? _____

_____

_____

_____

5. Are you pleased with your spiritual gifts? Why or why not? _____

_____

_____

_____

6. Have you ever been tempted to use a spiritual gift that is not yours? If so, give an example, and describe how well things went _____

_____

_____

_____

7. Have you ever given someone a gift only to discover they didn't like it, or they used it incorrectly? Does that experience help you understand your need to seek only God's will in using your gifts? How will you make sure He's in charge of your spiritual gifts? Be specific _____

_____

_____

_____

Chapter 18

GIVE UP EVERYTHING? ARE YOU CRAZY?

"Lord, you know I've accomplished much in my life so far. I have my Masters in Education (I know, pretty cool, huh?), I've briefly traveled abroad (I'm a well-rounded person), I've worked as a manager in a large international pharmaceutical company (pretty impressive, right?), I've traveled around the country training heads of companies (I actually impress MYSELF), I've seen great results from my teaching in elementary and middle school classrooms (What an asset to society, I am), and I've actually written books and had them published! I know you count me as one of your prized children, don't you, Lord?" I said as I finished my prayer.

As the day went on, it dawned on me that I had heard nothing but silence from the Lord regarding my question, so I pressed Him again to express what He thought of me. Finally, I sensed Him saying that I was to read Philippians 3:3-11. I opened my Bible, puzzled over what the Bible could possibly say about all my great achievements. Much to my shock, Paul sounded just like me, and I was in for a rude awakening! " ... *We rely on what Christ Jesus has done for us. We put no confidence in human effort, though I could have confidence in my own effort if anyone could. Indeed, if others have reason for confidence in their own efforts, I have even more! I was circumcised when I was eight days old. I am a pure-blooded citizen of Israel and a member of the tribe of Benjamin—a real Hebrew if there ever was one! I was a member of the Pharisees, who demand the strictest obedience to the Jewish law. I was so zealous that I harshly persecuted the church. And as for righteousness, I obeyed the law without fault. I once thought these things were valuable, but now I consider them worthless because of what Christ has done. Yes, everything else is worthless when compared with the infinite value of knowing Christ Jesus my Lord. For his sake I have discarded everything else, counting it all as garbage, so that I could gain Christ and become one with him. I no longer count on my own righteousness through obeying the law; rather, I become righteous through faith in Christ. For God's way of making us right with himself depends on faith. I want to know Christ and experience the mighty power that raised him from the dead. I want to suffer with him, sharing in his death, so that one way or another I will experience the resurrection from the dead!"*

"How could you possibly expect me to give up everything I've earned by all my hard work?" I agonized to the Lord. "All these accolades are true of me, and I deserve every one of them. I disagree with Paul—I think they ARE valuable!" I shouted. I slammed the Bible closed, absolutely incensed at the idea that what I had accomplished had no value to the Lord. In fact, His word said I had to look at all my portfolio of achievements as GARBAGE. Okay, so I equate garbage with smelly, obnoxious waste, and with things that I want kept far away from me so they can't negatively impact me. How could the Lord possibly call all my hard work garbage? I raced to the dictionary wondering if there was another definition I didn't know about, only to find that the definition for garbage included words like filth, rubbish, and dregs. One sentence stated, " . . . . anything that is contemptibly worthless, inferior, or vile." Now I was really upset! As I sat there with steam coming out of my ears, I began to sense the calming spirit of the Lord moving over my agitated emotions. As I settled down enough to actually listen to His quiet whisper, I realized He was showing me that I had not actually done any of these things on my own after all. Step by step, accomplishment after accomplishment, He showed me how HE was behind the opportunities I was given, the jobs I received, the chances to travel, the knowledge my company poured into me so I COULD train heads of companies, the money to travel, and even the wisdom I had to discern the best ways to teach and train children. He helped me understand that the accomplishments were not the problem—the problem was my **pride** over these accomplishments. Pride and arrogance were standing in the way of my ability to really know Jesus Christ! Because I thought I could take credit for everything on my resume, I was depending on my own knowledge and expertise to give me wisdom and guidance instead of the Lord. As God continued to illuminate my mind, I saw that as long as I was taking credit, I didn't really think I needed the Lord enough to seek Him with all my heart. Jeremiah 29:13 says, *"You will seek me and find me when you seek me with all your heart."* (NIV). Evidently, seeking with all my heart is the only way to really know Him, and the way to seek Him wholeheartedly is to depend on Him with every atom of my being. I realized I can't depend on Him in desperation, looking to Him for everything I need as long as I'm also depending on myself. My achievements were causing me to only recognize the Lord as a casual friend and helper rather than the love of my life, my only hope, my Savior, Redeemer, strength, and Guide. As the light dawned in my heart, I took my portfolio in my hands, gazed at it lovingly, and then placed it in the center of the trash can waiting for the garbage pick-up. I walked away without a backwards glance, my focus completely on the Lord now.

Much to my surprise, I suddenly felt a tap on my shoulder. As I turned around, there was the Lord, and He was reaching into the garbage can! He picked up my discarded portfolio and handed it back to me. In shock, I said, "Why are you giving this "garbage" back to me? You're the One who said it was smelly and offensive and that I needed to throw it away." The Lord smiled and said, "When used according to MY will and under MY supervision and guidance, these accomplishments are one of your greatest treasures! Now that you know you can't do anything of value in and of yourself, you are finally ready to effectively use all the resources I've placed in your life." Sure enough! As the days, weeks, and months went by, and I sought the Lord with everything in me, giving Him full credit for anything good that came out of my life, I began to notice Him using me in my areas of expertise! He used me to teach, to write, to train, and to utilize all the knowledge and instruction He made sure I received years ago. The best part was that I now depended completely on the Lord to show me how to use my abilities and experiences instead of trying to figure things out on my own. Not only did the pressure fall off my shoulders to be all things to all people and to have all the answers, but I was actually ABLE to meet the needs of the people God sent my way. I had wisdom that I never had before, strength to do the impossible, and outcomes that were beyond my comprehension. I just wished I had thrown my portfolio in the trash a long time ago!

----

1. List your own portfolio in detail. What do you think of it? _____
_____
_____
_____

2. How many of your accomplishments do you take most of the credit for? Why? _____
_____
_____
_____

3. What percentage of the time do you just reflexively jump into a situation and do what you've been trained to do, and what percentage of the time do you step back and ask the Lord for guidance? Explain
_____
_____
_____
_____

4. On a scale of 0-10, how difficult is it for you to ask the Lord for guidance when you're dealing with one of your areas of expertise? Should you have to? Why or why not? _____
_____
_____
_____

5. Has there ever been a time when you did what seemed right and appropriate in a situation you were well-trained for and it was the wrong thing to do? If so, give an example _____

_____

_____

_____

6. Do you think pride plays a part in how you view your portfolio? Is there a place for healthy pride, and if so, what does that look like? Do you sense any unhealthy pride attached to your perception of your portfolio? Explain _____

_____

_____

_____

7. On a scale of 0-10, how hard would it be for you to view all your accomplishments as equal to garbage? Would you do it if you knew it was the only way to really know Jesus Christ and to experience His mighty power for yourself? _____

_____

_____

_____

8. Has there ever been a time where you've seen God take your abilities and use them in ways that astonished you? If so, give an example

_____

_____

_____

_____

Chapter 19

WHAT DO YOU MEAN I'M THE "QUEEN OF DE'NILE"?

"Are you saying I'm not in touch with reality?" I demanded of my friend. "I disagree with you—I think I see things very clearly!" Muttering to myself about "With friends like that, who needs enemies?" I stomped off to my car, leaving my best friend shaking her head. On the way home, I rehearsed our conversation which had ended by my friend telling me that I was living in denial over pretty much everything in my life including my weight, my money-management style, and my current dating partner. "How dare she judge me," I fumed. "Who does she think she is pretending to know more about me than I do? I'm only a little overweight (pleasingly pump, I think it's called), and that's not my fault. I have a slow rate of metabolism and I hardly eat anything!" On and on, I ranted as I attempted to defend myself from her accusations. "I'm not that far in debt, and it's not my fault I make so little money! And, furthermore, my boyfriend is very nice to me and is a good man. Just because he doesn't go to church or read his Bible doesn't mean he's not just as good a Christian as she is!"

As I continued with my defensive attitude, it suddenly occurred to me to examine why I was so upset. "Why do I feel the need to defend myself?" I wondered. "Where is all this 'righteous' indignation coming from? If I'm right, why do I care what she thinks, and if I'm wrong, why can't I listen to her and carefully scrutinize what she's saying in light of Scripture? If I'm not sure who's right, why am I so opposed to the idea of checking out my ideas, motives, and behavior?" Little by little, I began to understand that I WANTED to live my life in a hidden way according to whatever felt good at the time, and I didn't WANT anyone to hold me accountable. I desired all the benefits of pretending to be godly while secretly living exactly the way I perceived I needed to in order to be happy. Shocked, as understanding crept into my heart, I began rethinking our conversation once again. First of all, I knew deep down inside of me that I WAS overweight and that my eating habits WERE the cause of my weight gain. I knew that if God were visibly eating every meal with me, I would eat differently in an effort to please Him. Even though technically He IS eating every meal with me, I was able to block out that thought and pretend He couldn't see my indiscretions. You see, in the actual moment when I saw or thought of food, or when it was placed in front of me, I desperately desired that extra piece of bread, gooey dessert, salty chips, or a high-caloric beverage. I was so sure that indulging my cravings would help me feel better, and, at least for a few minutes, it DID! That is, until I got on the scales and faced the high numbers appearing between my feet. I found myself unable to deny my appetite for too much food or the wrong kinds of food so I developed an image-management routine for anyone who questioned me, or to use if I just felt guilty and needed to defend myself even to myself: "I just haven't lost all my weight from my pregnancy yet; I gain weight if I just LOOK at food; I have large bones so I need to carry more weight to look healthy; I'm genetically pre-disposed to gaining weight; I'm joining the gym next month just to tone up a little and then I'll be fine," etc. Now, as I looked at my behavior and words, I realized that my friend was absolutely right—I was living smack dab in the middle of denial!

Forcing myself to continue reviewing the conversation with my friend, I focused on the next issue she brought up—my money-management style. As much as I hated to admit it, I knew I was out of control when it came to spending money. If I saw something I wanted, I began to covet it, to think about how it would make my life better, to remind myself what a good deal it was, and to picture it on me or in my house until I was finally convinced I couldn't live without it. I wanted to budget. I planned to budget. I even prayed about my budget needs, but I couldn't, or didn't want to curb my desires for the things that struck my fancy. I knew I was playing with fire because my income didn't match my spending habits, but the idea of living within my means was too upsetting to contemplate. Total self-discipline would mean I would not be able to use spending as a means of comfort, and then what would I do? Once again, I pretended to everyone around me that I had things under control: "Once I get my income tax return, I'll be okay; I'm planning on attending a money-management seminar at my church; I haven't bought anything new for a long time; everything I bought was on sale; I only buy what I really need." Shame overcame me as I saw how deeply my thought process was rooted in denial.

Finally, I thought about my boyfriend. That was the most painful subject of all because I so desperately wanted to be in a committed relationship. If I were honest with myself, I knew that my boyfriend wasn't a Christian, but I couldn't seem to find a good Christian guy, or so I told myself. "I'm sure he'll go to church with me one of these days and he'll get saved soon," I assuaged my guilt. "I won't get serious with him until I know he's really a Christian," I soothed my conscience. "I'll ask him if he'll talk with my pastor, or maybe he'd like to come to my small group with me." Suddenly, it hit me that I was doing it again—I was wallowing in denial! The truth was that I had never broached the subject of church with him or even told him I was a Christian because I was afraid it would turn him off. I was far more involved with him emotionally and physically than I had allowed myself to recognize because I so longed for someone to "love" me. I realized I had no intentions of rocking the boat, and that I was just selfishly indulging in a relationship that made me feel good about myself. I began to see myself from God's perspective and it was ugly! I had pretended for years, I had hidden behind facades, and I had indulged in constant image-management all with the intent to cover my sins and live life according to my own rules. I would never have admitted that truth to myself, nor done these things openly, but living in denial allowed me to turn my face away from reality, at least, until my friend confronted me.

As I grieved over the mess in my life brought about by my desire to hide from the truth, I reached for my dusty Bible on the night stand. I couldn't read it too often or too carefully and still stay in denial, so it hadn't been opened for a while. As I flipped through the pages, this verse in 1 John 1:6 caught my eye, "*So we are lying if we say we have fellowship with God but go on living in spiritual darkness; we are not practicing the truth.*" Oh, the pain I felt in my heart as I realized I had been actually lying to myself, to others, and to the Lord with all my pretending and image-management. I saw denial for what it was, "a psychological process by which painful truths are not admitted into an individual's consciousness" (dictionary definition). Sobered, as the truth of God's word hit me between the eyes, I cautiously peered back into the Bible fearful of what else the Lord wanted to show me. Sure enough, He was very harsh in His judgment of people who choose to live in denial. 2 Timothy 3:5 says, "*They will act religious, but they will reject the power that could make them godly. Stay away from people like that!*" Since God is only that harsh for a good reason, I looked more closely at this verse until I realized that by choosing to living in denial, I was refusing to turn to God for help in overcoming my harmful desires. Instead of trusting Him to chart my course and give me strength, I was actually **rejecting** His power that would have made me godly as I longed to be. My heart broke when I saw how I had damaged my life and hurt my Lord, and I begged Him to give me some hope for my future. Of course He did, and it was right next to the verse that talked about living in darkness. He went on to say in 1 John 1:7, "*But if we are living in the light, as God is in the light, then we have fellowship with each other, and the blood of Jesus, his Son, cleanses us from all sin.*" My heart lifted in joy to realize that God DOES offer a way out of denial. Instead of living in the darkness of denial and pretending, I could actually live in the light of honesty and transparency. Ephesians 4:25 showed me how: "*So stop telling lies. Let us tell our neighbors the truth, for we are all parts of the same body.*"

"Wow!" I thought. "How simple! Just tell the truth to myself and to everyone else, and I'll be home free." At the thought of coming out of denial and telling the truth, though, I shrank back inside of myself, scared to death at how difficult it would be to cease wrapping myself in the safe and comforting cloak of denial. "What if people don't like me?" I whimpered. "What if I can't lose the weight and people look down on me? What if I don't get to buy the things I want? Will I still be happy?

What if I'm just left alone with no companionship? I KNOW I couldn't handle THAT scenario!" God lovingly pointed to the verses in Colossians 3:9-10, "*Don't lie to each other, for you have stripped off your old sinful nature and all its wicked deeds. Put on your new nature, and be renewed as you learn to know your Creator and become like him.*" I exhaled in relief realizing that God Himself would be helping me tell the truth as I chose to become more and more like Him. I turned my hands up to Him letting Him know that nothing in my life would ever again be deliberately hidden from Him, and I would never knowingly withhold anything from Him. I felt so clean and fresh and renewed in my spirit—well, that is, until I heard a whisper from the Lord. "You want me to what?" I gasped. "You want me to call my friend and tell her everything I've been learning? No, no, no, it's too soon," I pleaded. "I'm not ready yet to divulge the depths of my denial."

"There's no time like the present, you say?" I repeated to the Lord in disbelief. He didn't respond, so in resignation, yet with a tingly sort of anticipation, I reached to dial my friend and start the process of learning to "walk in the light as He is in the light." Thank goodness, He'll be with me as long as I STAY in the light!

----

1. Do you think you have any areas of denial in your life? If so, what are they? _____

_____

_____

_____

2. If you said, "Yes," what causes you to walk in denial instead of honesty?

_____

_____

_____

_____

3. How would your closest friends answer this question about you? If you disagreed with their answers, how hard would it be for you to listen to their perspectives? Explain _____

_____

_____

_____

4. Do you have any friends who you feel comfortable enough with to be honest and transparent? If so, how does it feel to have no secrets in your life once you've been open with them? Explain _____

_____

_____

_____

5. Does the idea of joining an accountability group scare you? Why or why not? Would you be willing to join one if the end result would enable you to completely walk in the light? _____

_____

_____

_____

6. Do you think you'd act or speak any differently if the Lord were actually visible to you? Why or why not? _____

_____

_____

_____

7. Why do you think it's so easy for most Christians to slip into denial rather than choosing to be honest? _____

_____

_____

_____

Chapter 20

WHAT DO YOU MEAN I'M JUST A LUMP OF CLAY?

I overheard an acquaintance make that statement about me one day ("Well, what can you expect since she's just a lump of clay?") and the hackles rose on the back of my neck! What do you mean," I challenged her. "I know the Bible says I was made from dust which is obviously similar to clay (Ecclesiastus 3:20, "*All go to the same place; all come from dust, and to dust all return*." And God, Himself, says in Psalm 103:14, "*For he knows how weak we are; he remembers we are only dust*.), but I'm actually far more valuable than you're insinuating. Look at all the things I've accomplished in my lifetime, and see how many people respect what I have to say and offer. I make a good salary and my company couldn't get along without me. To tell you the truth, most people in my circle of influence couldn't manage without my knowledge and expertise, even my family. I'm the glue that holds things together. I'm well-educated, self-disciplined, and motivated to learn and grow in all areas of my life. Just because I will eventually decompose into dirt again doesn't mean I don't have tremendous value and worth because of how hard I've worked to be successful."

Seeing that I had silenced my would-be persecutor, I packed up my briefcase and left for home. Later that evening as I was reflecting on my brilliant defense of my numerous achievements, I picked up my Bible for my daily evening reading. Much to my shock and horror, the passage designated for today was from Jeremiah 18:2-6, "*Go down to the potter's shop, and I will speak to you there*." So I did as he told me and found the *potter working at his wheel. But the jar he was making did not turn out as he had hoped, so he crushed it into a lump of clay again and started over. Then the Lord gave me this message: "O Israel, can I not do to you as this potter has done to his clay? As the clay is in the potter's hand, so are you in my hand."*

"No!" I shouted, quickly covering my mouth so I wouldn't waken the kids. "God doesn't mean what it sounds like He's saying. He couldn't possibly be serious! Look at my brilliant mind, my ability to get things done when no one else can, my great people skills, and my organizational strengths. God would never want to crush me and start over again. Why would I even pretend to give Him permission to do that? I don't want to be in His "hand" if that's what it would mean." I stormed off to bed, too tired and upset to sort out my emotions, and too scared to consider the whole clay and potter analogy.

The next evening I picked up my Bible again hoping for a nice Psalm to soothe my troubled mind. Wouldn't you know it! The selection was for Isaiah 45:9, "*What sorrow awaits those who argue with their Creator. Does a clay pot argue with its maker? Does the clay dispute with the one who shapes it, saying, 'Stop, you're doing it wrong!' Does the pot exclaim, 'How clumsy can you be?'*" Slamming my Bible shut, I looked up at the ceiling and said, "That's not funny, Lord! Are you trying to tell me that I have no more value than an inanimate object like a lump of clay? How insulting! I thought I was made in your image; I thought I was your precious child." Hearing no answer, I sighed, reached for the light switch, and trudged off to bed.

The next night, I guardedly picked up my Bible, tempted to just pick out a verse I was familiar with instead of doing the usual study I had selected months ago. A hint of curiosity overcame me, though, and I decided to just take a peek at the selection for today. The word "potter" caught my eye, and before I could stop myself, I was reading the verses in Isaiah 29:16 "*How foolish can you be? He is the Potter, and he is certainly greater than you, the clay! Should the created thing say of the one who made it, 'He didn't make me'? Does a jar ever say, 'The potter who made me is stupid'?*" Incredulously, I looked at the study guide wondering why I had ever chosen this ridiculous book in the first place. "First of all," I exclaimed in disgust, "the writer is stuck in the Old Testament, and secondly, he's trying to make me feel like I'm not very important." Pushing back the thought that God was trying to speak to me, I stuck the book under a pile of textbooks on my desk and tried to put those worrisome thoughts out of my head.

I had no peace all the next day, though, and fragments of the verses I'd read kept running through my mind making it hard for me to concentrate. To make matters worse, I lost a sale I'd been counting on, and my boss gave me a lower review than I was expecting. As I fell into my desk chair at home that night, my eyes zeroed in on the study guide sticking out from under the books where I had shoved it. I made a firm decision on the spot. "I'll just see where the scripture reference is from," I told myself, "and if it's from the Old Testament, I'm not reading it tonight!" Much to my great relief, the verses for today were from Romans 9:20-21, and I started reading with great anticipation only to stare in disbelief at the words, "*No, don't say that. Who are you, a mere human being, to argue with God? Should the thing that was created say to the one who created it, "Why have you made me like this?" When a potter makes jars out of clay, doesn't he have a right to use the same lump of clay to make one jar for decoration and another to throw garbage into?*" I couldn't ignore the Lord's words any longer, and I bowed my head in defeat. "Do you often use objects to compare us to, Lord, or did you just want to humiliate me these last four nights?" I questioned querulously. "I can't believe I've never read all these verses before or realized You said these things about me." The thought came to me to check the cross-references in my Bible, and with much trepidation, I began to read the verses suggested in my margin. "*But can the ax boast greater power than the person who uses it? Is the saw greater than the person who saws? Can a rod strike unless a hand moves it? Can a wooden cane walk by itself?*" Isaiah 10:15. By this point, I was truly frustrated. "Lord, I fail to find the humor in these verses," I snarled. "Are you saying that I should have no thoughts or feelings about ANYTHING? Am I of no more worth to you than just being a mindless tool for You to use?"

Upset beyond comprehension, I turned to head for my room when I sensed the Lord prompting me to read more of the verses in my margin starting with James 4:14, "*How do you know what your life will be like tomorrow? Your life is like the morning fog—it's here a little while, then it's gone.*" The next reference was from 1 Peter 1:24. "*As the Scriptures say, "People are like grass; their beauty is like a flower in the field. The grass withers and the flower fades.*" Suddenly, a light came on in my brain, and I began to realize that the Lord wasn't trying to debase me or take away my dignity. Instead, He was attempting to show me that I have no more ability than grass, or fog, or an axe, or the hated clay analogy to do anything of value or lasting worth on my own! He was showing me that I had a choice to let Him completely run my life with His hands on every part of my being like a potter does with clay, or I could keep using my own logic to guide my days. He was utilizing the strongest language and word pictures possible to show me my foolishness in thinking I had achieved any success on my own whatsoever. As I hung my head in shame, realizing that I was taking credit for my dear Savior's work in my life, I saw these words from 2 Timothy 2:20-21, "*In a wealthy home some utensils are made of gold and silver, and some are made of wood and clay. The expensive utensils are used for special occasions, and the cheap ones are for everyday use. If you keep yourself pure, you will be a special utensil for honorable use. Your life will be clean, and you will be ready for the Master to use you for every good work.*" It struck me that God was giving me the chance to choose which type of utensil I wanted to be. If I continued to follow my own desires and thoughts, I would cause irreversible damage that would negatively affect my usefulness for fulfilling God's plans.

Completely willing to listen to the Lord's voice now, and eager to see what else He had to say to me, I opened my Bible to 2 Corinthians 4:7, "*We now have this light shining in our hearts, but we ourselves are like fragile clay jars containing this great treasure. This makes it clear that our great power is from God, not from ourselves.*" Full illumination burst into my heart and I realized that, in and of myself, I AM nothing more than a lump of clay. The good news is that God has poured the essence of Himself into my body, my jar of clay, and HE is the one that is making me successful through His wonderful power in my life. I'm only the vessel, not the treasure itself! "I get it," I declared to the Lord with my hands raised to the ceiling. "It's all about YOU, not me! Yes, you may crush me and start over again because you are the wise potter with perfect hands that know exactly how to shape me into the best masterpiece you desire ("*For we are God's masterpiece. He has created us anew in Christ Jesus, so we can do the good things he planned for us long ago.*" Ephesians 2:10)." Wanting to make sure I was no longer resisting the potter, I fell to my knees with my forehead touching the family room floor looking as much like a lump of clay as possible. Sure enough, I sensed the excited, skillful hands of the most perfect Potter who ever lived beginning the process of reshaping my newly soft and pliable heart. I began to sing, "Have Thine own way, Lord! Have Thine own way! Thou art the Potter, I am the clay. Mold me and make me after Thy will, while I am waiting, yielded and still." (author: Adelaide Pollard). The best part of the story is that God will keep working with His "clay child" and never give up until I'm the perfect piece of pottery He envisioned when I was born! ("*And I am certain that God, who began the good work within you, will continue his work until it is finally finished on the day when Christ Jesus returns.*" Philippians 1:6).

----

1. Did it surprise you how many times God refers to His children using inanimate objects? Why or why not? _____

_____

_____

_____

2. Do you struggle with the seeming contradictions in the Bible claiming that we are both a lump of clay and God's masterpiece? How do you resolve those different descriptions of a Christian? _____

_____

_____

_____

3. How do you feel about God's rejection of your own thought process having any value or worth in and of itself? What percentage of the time do you spend following your own wisdom versus seeking God's wisdom? Why? _____

_____

_____

_____

4. How do you feel about being compared to a lump of clay? Would you consider allowing the "Potter" to treat you as a lump of clay? Why or why not? _____

_____

_____

_____

5. How do you think your life would change if you actually submitted to the controlling yet perfect hands of the "Potter?" Explain _____

_____

_____

_____

6. Do you know anyone who appears to have fully embraced their role as a lump of clay? If so, who? What do you think of that person? Do they tempt you to submit to the Potter's hands or do they turn you away from that idea? Explain _____

_____

_____

_____

Chapter 21

No Thanks, I Don't Need Your Help!

I settled into my seat at church a few minutes early and spent the time perusing the program. On the back page, I found an advertisement for a new support group starting up on Monday nights for women and Thursday nights for men. Curious, I read further to find out these meetings were actually accountability groups where attendees would be encouraged to share praises and prayer requests while being as transparent as possible about their activities and feelings during the previous week as they "check in" with the other members. The stated goal was to help each person seek the Lord in a more obedient manner through asking others to hold them accountable and to pray for them. I laid down my program in disgust wondering what the church was coming to. "Is this some sort of touchy-feely group, or are these attendees just weak people who can't get their acts together?" I wondered. "Who needs to waste time at get-togethers like these when all it takes is a good dose of self-discipline to get on the right track?" I muttered to myself. "I think there are lots of people with too much time on their hands! Besides, these meetings sound like a breeding ground for gossip. There's no way I'm going to spend my precious downtime being psychoanalyzed by a bunch of amateur counselors!" With that final thought, I turned my attention to the platform where the worship leader was asking us to stand and begin singing.

After the service, my best friend rushed up to me all excited about the new support groups and eager to help me sign up for the next Monday night. With all the patience I could muster, I put her off and managed to escape without signing up. "Why do people WANT to go to these kinds of groups?" I fumed. "They sure don't sound very biblical to me!" At that thought, I suddenly wondered what the Bible DID say about support groups. "Surely God is perfectly capable of working one-on-one with His children," I assured myself. "There's no good reason I need to feel guilty for bowing out of this kind of torture." Those kinds of thoughts sustained me all the way home and right up to the point where I began searching God's Word for His perspective. It didn't take long before my eyes fell on this verse in James 5:16, and in shock and dismay, I began to read: *"Confess your sins to each other and pray for each other so that you may be healed. The earnest prayer of a righteous person has great power and produces wonderful results."* With a sinking heart, I begged God to show me why He wrote this command in His Word. "Why do I have to tell my faults to other people and have THEM pray for me before I can be healed?" I railed. "That doesn't make any sense to me!" Well, the Lord wasn't finished with me yet, and as I flipped over to Acts to see how the early church handled things, I came across chapter 19, verse 18, *"Many of those who believed now came and openly confessed their evil deeds."* (NIV). I shuddered to think of having to "openly" confess MY evil deeds, and I wondered why that was necessary. My fingers of their own volition wandered over to Romans 10:9-10, *"If you confess with your mouth that Jesus is Lord and believe in your heart that God raised him from the dead, you will be saved. For it is by believing in your heart that you are made right with God, and it is by confessing with your mouth that you are saved."* I began to realize that there's something about speaking out loud that is critical to our spiritual well-being. Evidently, speaking out the truth, even about our sins, is part of how we process and accept the truth about ourselves whether it's painful truth or glorious truth.

Now the Lord had my attention, and I began to research the Bible more to see if there were any other places where God tells me to be open and accountable to others. Of course there were, since God generally repeats Himself when He gives a command. Galatians 6:1 was the next verse to catch my attention, *"Dear brothers and sisters, if another believer is overcome by some sin, you who are godly should gently and humbly help that person back onto the right path. And be careful not to fall into the same temptation yourself."* I sat back in astonishment as I began to understand how important it was for me to not only be accountable to others, but to take an active role in helping hold OTHERS accountable. 1 Thessalonians 5:11, 14 were the next verses that caught my attention, *"So encourage each other and build each other up, just as you are already doing. Brothers and sisters, we urge you to warn those who are lazy. Encourage those who are timid. Take tender care of those who are weak. Be patient with everyone."*

"How come I never saw these verses before?" I wondered. "Forcing myself to be open and accountable to others, and holding those same people accountable seems to be a key part of helping me grow closer to the Lord, and I didn't even know it!" Frustrated that I had overlooked such an important component of spiritual growth, I continued to search the Scriptures finding such verses as Hebrews 3:13-14, *"You must warn each other every day, while it is still "today," so that none of you will be deceived by sin and hardened against God.",* and Hebrews 12:15, *"Look after each other so that none of you fails to receive the grace of God. Watch out that no poisonous root of bitterness grows up to trouble you, corrupting many."*

As I pondered all these verses, I began to feel a sense of rebellion cropping up in my heart. "I don't WANT to tell others my faults," I chafed. "It's so embarrassing and humiliating to be vulnerable. What if they judge me? What if they tell others about my problems? What if I'm the only one with those particular faults and they don't have patience with me? What if I try to hold someone else accountable and I do it wrongly, or they won't accept my help and perspective?" God patiently began to help me understand that while any of my fears could very possibly occur since Christians are all human and prone to sin, I still needed to reach out to others and choose to be vulnerable according to God's command. Desperate to understand and yet so fearful of obeying, I thought about why God would command something so hard and painful. I realized that if I can't even see my own face without the help of a camera or a mirror, why did I think I could accurately "see" my inner self? I saw that God gave **others** the perspective on **me** that I desperately needed as a way to knit us all together in a loving, united family. I can't grow spiritually without the help of my brothers and sisters because of my internal blindedness! As I thought about that piece of truth, I understood that I tend to overlook, explain away, and rationalize my faults until I'm incapable of seeing the reality that they exist and that they are destroying me! Only with the help of others can I find out the truth about myself and bring it to the Lord for the help I need to overcome each fault.

Amazed at the wisdom of the Lord and His creative ways to bind us all together, and His plan to keep us humble and patient with each other, I slowly reached for my phone and dialed the number of the church. When the phone was picked up on the other end, I shakily gave out my name and information and asked to be signed up for the new support group starting next Monday night. "God help me," I whispered, as I hung up the phone, and just then, peace filled my heart. As hard as it would be to walk into that support group, I knew God was all for it and would give me the strength and wisdom I needed to make choosing honesty, transparency, and humbleness something to be sought after instead of feared. A smile began to form as I pictured the look on my best friend's face when I showed up at an accountability group of all places!

----

1. How do you feel about support/accountability groups? Explain

_____

_____

_____

_____

2. Have you ever attended an accountability group? If so, how did your experience turn out? _____

_____

_____

_____

3. How do you feel about being held accountable, and being transparent and honest with a safe group of people? Were you surprised to find out Scripture commands us to live in this type of community with other Christians? Explain _____

_____

_____

_____

4. How have you handled the part of holding other people accountable? Is that activity harder or easier for you than being accountable yourself? Why? _____

_____

_____

_____

5. Have you ever opened up to the wrong person, or shared your heart only to be rejected or judged or criticized? Have you ever had someone break your confidence? If any of these things have happened to you, give examples _____

_____

_____

_____

6. How hard is it for you to ever try to be held accountable again if you've experienced some sort of betrayal or felt unsafe? Explain _____

_____

_____

_____

7. Have you ever been the "unsafe" person in an accountability situation? If so, why did you choose to be unsafe? Does your own behavior make it harder for you to trust others to be safe? Why or why not? _____

_____

_____

_____

8. Perhaps the greatest gift we can give another person is to treasure their secrets and protect their faults from the judging eyes of others. What do you think about that statement? _____

_____

_____

_____

9. Now that you know God commands us to be in accountability with other Christians, are you willing to do so even if you've had bad experiences in the past? Why or why not? _____

_____

_____

_____

10. What role does pride play in your choice to be held accountable? Are you ever tempted to pretend, or only share about certain areas of your life? Have you ever been tempted to hide a particular area of your life from everyone, even hoping God doesn't see it? How did you handle those temptations? _____

_____

_____

_____

11. Have you ever succumbed to the temptation to hide? Did you feel safer hiding? Did you feel any other emotions in your hiding? If so, what emotions? Did you find good coming out of your hiding? Did your hiding help or hurt others? How? _____

_____

_____

_____

Chapter 22

THANK GOODNESS FOR COMMON SENSE!

"Why are so many people lacking in common sense?" I muttered to myself. "This world would be a far better place if people would just use their brains! Look at those people running around outside in the freezing cold with just socks and sandals on," I fumed, "and look how those people are ignoring their kids. Why all kinds of bad things could happen to those children and the parents would be devastated. They'd probably blame everyone else for their pain instead of realizing they could have easily prevented their heartache. And then there are the people who don't take good care of themselves and end up getting sick, missing work, and feeling miserable. All these negative events could be avoided if they just had an ounce of common sense!"

Continuing my running commentary to myself on the sad state of the world, I almost missed the quiet whisper from the Lord. "What IS common sense?" He said gently. "How do you know if someone is using common sense or not? Is it possible that 'common sense' means different things to different people? Are you basing your conclusions on your flawed thought process, or is there a book out there somewhere that you're following? I'm just wondering because I'VE never mentioned common sense anywhere in MY book, and I thought that was the book you're patterning your life after." I sputtered in shock and disbelief as the soft voice faded away. "What do you mean, Lord?" I asked incredulously. "Everyone knows what common sense is and that it's the most safe, logical, and efficient way to guide our daily activities. You know, 'Experience is the best teacher' even though it IS a hard taskmaster at times. Even the dictionary has a definition for common sense: 'sound practical judgment that is independent of specialized knowledge, training, or the like; normal native intelligence', and, of course, the dictionary is always reliable. I understand that You can't be bothered worrying about every little action and word of all your kids, so common sense is what we humans use, well some of us "WISER" ones, to handle these daily needs for quick answers."

Sure that I had convinced the Lord of something that seemed so basic and right to me, I picked up my thread of frustrated thoughts on the lack of common sense in the people around me from where I left off when the Lord interrupted me, and went out to mow the lawn. Of course, I had on my steel-toed boots to make sure I was safe around the lawn mower, and I had on my safely goggles to prevent any flying stones from hitting me in the eyes, and I wore gloves to make sure I didn't get any blisters. As I was mowing, I began to hear the voice of the Lord again in spite of the loud noise of the motor. He said, "Why are you so sold on this common sense idea you keep railing about? I think you trust your own interpretation of the right thing to do more than you do Me." ("*If you need wisdom, ask our generous God, and he will give it to you. He will not rebuke you for asking.*" James 1:5) "My wisdom is MY answer to your longing for common sense to rule."

Surprised at the Lord's question, and more than a little perturbed that He wouldn't let the topic go, I allowed myself to ponder my love affair with common sense. Much to my dismay, I realized it came from FEAR! I was afraid that if I wasn't careful enough to follow all the safety rules and all the guidelines put forth by very smart and/or experienced people, and all the lessons I'VE learned on what not to do, I would be fair game for Satan to haunt me with guilt if something bad happened. I realized that I had convinced myself that if I tried my best and did everything I could to stay safe and keep those I loved safe, I would at least be free of guilt in my pain when something went wrong. I began to see that the flaws in my thinking were believing I could prevent others from thinking negatively about me, or worse, charging me legally with neglect, AND that I could thwart Satan instead of understanding that he can easily flood me with guilt no matter how hard I try to do everything right. He'll always find something he can blame me for. Even God calls him *"The accuser of our brothers and sisters—the one who accuses them before our God day and night."* (Revelation 12:10b). I can only overcome Satan's power, deception, and influence over me by calling on the name of the Lord to strengthen and protect me, not by my own strength, and certainly not by my very weak, fallible, and vulnerable thought process (*"So humble yourselves before God. Resist the devil, and he will flee from you."* James 4:7). "How did I forget that truth?" I wondered.

I suddenly saw that I was following a worldly expression that people falsely believe comes from the Bible that says, "God helps those who help themselves." It seemed so right and logical to believe that God expected me to do my part by trying my very best to do everything as perfectly as possible, and then God would come along and finish up whatever I wasn't able to complete or just missed. "But God," I remonstrated, "I know you want me to work hard and to perform well and to plan my life so I don't make any mistakes, right?" As I carefully mowed the lawn in nice straight lines, and waited for the Lord to speak again, words to a song floated through my mind, "Without Him I could do nothing, without Him I'd surely fail." (Author: Mylon R. Lefevre). "No, that can't be true," I blurted out. "I KNOW I'm right! I KNOW I can figure out these small decisions and do them correctly. What does that song mean when it uses words like 'nothing', and 'surely fail'?" By now I was really upset and fuming, and my rows in the lawn were starting to become wavy. "Why did you give me a mind, Lord, if you didn't expect me to use it? My experiences, those with both good and bad consequences, outfitted me with the capability of reasoning out the best way to handle the daily choices that face me. Even other people notice that I continually use common sense to guide my life, and they praise me for it. What's that you're saying, Lord? Are you telling me that every circumstance in my life is not identical, and that identical decisions based on my experiences will most likely produce a different and possibly negative result? Are you saying that you want the results to be the ones YOU designed for me, not what common sense may luckily or fatefully bring me? Am I not allowing you to get a word in edgewise when I'm following my own perceptions? Is my fear turning me into a control freak?" (*"I [Jesus] can do nothing on my own. I judge as*

God tells me. Therefore, my judgment is just, because I carry out the will of the one who sent me, not my own will." John 5:30)

By now I was so upset, and the lawn was such a mess that I turned off the mower and went back into the house. God wasn't letting up on me, though, and He reminded me that my thought process was infected with a virus at my birth when my sin nature came alive. Then, just like that, before I even had a chance to take my shoes off and sit down, a verse popped into my mind, "*All of us, like sheep, have strayed away. We have left God's paths to follow our own.*" (Isaiah 53:6). As I collapsed on my chair, I ruminated on that picture in my mind: "ALL" is a pretty encompassing word, and sheep are really dumb animals! I pictured them all meandering off the right pathway to cavort in the grass, never realizing they were headed toward a cliff. I didn't like being compared to a sheep. "Are you saying I can't make ANY decisions on my own, Lord? I have to run EVERY decision past you? That behavior doesn't make any sense, though, because I'd never get anything done! You're too slow in answering my questions, and besides, I don't always know what it is you're telling me to do. It's just easier to do what seems right to me based on past experiences. What's that you're saying? I'm giving in to my lazy mind that wants to do what it wants to do WHEN it wants to do things? I'm just trying to control the outcome of all my decisions? I'm just trying to make everything turn out for my comfort so I have the kind of life that I think is best for me?" (God wants just the opposite for me—"*My old self has been crucified with Christ. It is no longer I who live, but Christ lives in me. So I live in this earthly body by trusting in the Son of God, who loved me and gave himself for me.*" Galatians 2:20)

Filled with horror and disbelieve, I sat there in shock. How could everything that seemed so true and safe and right to my way of thinking be completely wrong? How could the Lord possibly want me to ask His guidance and direction on everything I said and did? I just knew He couldn't really mean for me to follow those guidelines. Why if I did, I'd NEVER get anything done and I'd always be totally confused. ("*And so, dear brothers and sisters, I plead with you to give your bodies to God because of all he has done for you. Let them be a living and holy sacrifice—the kind he will find acceptable. This is truly the way to worship him. Don't copy* *the behavior and customs of this world, but let God transform you into a new person **by changing the way you think**. Then you will learn to know God's will for you, which is good and pleasing and perfect."* Romans 12:1-2) {Bolding added}.

My total frustration at this point threatened to send me into a tailspin until the thought came to search the Bible and see how godly people lived their lives. Surely, when God was speaking to them, He used common sense principles to direct their lives, and surely they would never obey anything else. My Bible was sitting within easy reach of my chair and I started at the beginning. Interestingly enough, I came across Eve almost immediately and read her discussion with Satan over the Tree of the Knowledge of Good and Evil. Suddenly, it dawned on me that right here, in the beginning, was where the problem started. It was SATAN who got Eve to begin trying to reason things out with her own thought process and he's been at it in every human's life since! Up to that point, Eve had just "trusted in the Lord with all her heart and not depended on her own understanding. She had sought HIS will in all she did, and He showed her which path to take." (Proverbs 3:5-6) After she chose to listen to Satan's reasoning, though, she failed miserably and, as they say, the rest is history. Then there was the story of Sarah and Abraham attempting to follow God's plan using their own logic. They decided that since Sarah wasn't able to conceive, or so she thought, they should use Hagar to produce a son for Abraham. The long-range negative consequences of that bit of "common sense" are being felt throughout the world at this very moment, thousands of years after the fact!

I sat back in my chair, overcome with these new insights. "God, can using common sense be the equivalent of listening to Satan?" I mused. "Is it possible that what seems so good to me, just like it did to Eve and to Abraham and Sarah, is actually as damaging and destructive to follow as it was for them? (*"There is a way that seems right to a man, but in the end it leads to death."* Proverbs 14:12) "But what's the answer then, Lord?" I pleaded. "Do you want me to go against everything that seems right and logical and safe? Do you want me to cross the street without looking? Do you want me to put my kids in the car without safety restraints? Do you want me to take them to the park and then just let them go play without watching over them? Do you want me to trust strangers? Do you want me to leave a sharp knife in front of a small child while I go answer the doorbell? Do you want me to turn my back on common sense completely?"

Not hearing a response, I turned to my Bible again and began to read accounts of Noah building a huge boat far from water in a place where there had never been rain. I realized he did it just because God told him to, not because it made any sense whatsoever. I read about Abraham who took his only child up on a mountain to kill him just because God told him to, never mind that killing your child is against every law God has ever given! Then there was Gideon who took three hundred men into battle against an enemy comprised of tens of thousands of soldiers just because God told him to, even though the odds were stacked against him per common sense's rules. I went on to read about David as a teenager going out to fight a 9-foot giant with a slingshot! Common sense would have told him to take an AK-47 or at least a bazooka, OR to run for the hills! I read the account of Daniel praying out his open window even though it would cost him a night in the lion's den. That decision certainly wasn't one of his smarter ones. The list of people in the Bible who ignored common sense in their behavior or who were told by the Lord to directly go against all human reasoning went on and on. The New Testament had its share, too. There were Peter and John who continued to preach even after being warned of the consequences by the government agents and religious leaders. Of course, there was Paul who never did the "wise" thing and ended up being whipped and thrown into prison numerous times. The rest of the disciples, and all the early church Christians appeared to flirt with danger every chance they got, rarely stopping to consider the consequences. They were driven to please the Lord at all costs, and the way to please the Lord didn't appear to coincide very often with the path of common sense.

Numbly, I closed my Bible and began to reflect on my findings. The light finally began to dawn on my confusion stemming from fear, distrust, and stubbornness. I realized that, while God guides us at times to follow the ways of common sense, He reserves the right to bypass those laws at any given moment. We will never know when He might

have a "higher" purpose in mind and direct us to follow Him no matter what our brains, or others, may say. The key is to always ask Him what He wants us to do in every situation and never take anything for granted. I realized that my need to control my circumstances prevented me from hearing the voice of the Lord, and from experiencing the miracles of slaying a giant, or saving my family from a flood, or watching the rout of thousands of soldiers at the hands of a tiny army, or seeing angels close lion's mouths, or watching prison gates open of their own volition, or being left for dead and then resurrected, as Paul was, to continue serving the Lord. I realized at that moment that I had a choice. I could live my safe, controlled life, feeling good about my decisions, even though I saw mistakes, regrets, unhappiness, offense, failure, and other negative consequences coming from them, or I could throw caution to the wind and live the wild, crazy, God-honoring, miracle-producing, joy-supplying, treasure-yielding life God had planned for me when He created me. What a choice I was facing! Suddenly, the decision seemed easy when I realized I would miss out on everything that really mattered to me, and that I would make all kinds of mistakes negatively affecting me and all those I loved, if I continued to let common sense thwart God's higher goals. ("*Anyone who builds on that foundation* [Jesus Christ] *may use a variety of materials—gold, silver, jewels, wood, hay, or straw. But on the judgment day, fire will reveal what kind of work each builder has done. The fire will show if a person's work has any value. If the work survives, that builder will receive a reward. But if the work is burned up, the builder will suffer great loss. The builder will be saved, but like someone barely escaping through a wall of flames.*" 1Corinthians 3:12-15) The idea of my life having such value and purpose began to look better and more attractive the more I thought about it, even if it meant I had to let go of my fears and need to control, and actually TRUST the Lord. Finally, I took a deep breath, gathered up the remnants of my desperate need to be in charge, and slowly handed the reins of my life into God's safe, dependable hands. ("*For I can do everything through Christ, who gives me strength.*" Philippians 4:13)

Well, my first test came when I looked out the window and saw the mess of my lawn-mowing attempts. There were the nice, straight lines, followed by increasingly wavy lines, and finally the abrupt halt of the lawn mower right in the middle of my yard. Quickly, I pulled on my shoes, intent on fixing the damage before anyone could see it, when the voice of the Lord came loud and clear. "I want you to just leave it," He said. "But Lord, what will the neighbors think? Besides, the lawn mower is right in a place where the kids cut through my yard on their way home from school. They could get hurt on it, or break it if they play around with it." Again, the prompting of the Lord was very strong. "Just leave it and trust me," He whispered. Fuming, I plopped down in my chair again, realizing that doing things the Lord's way when it didn't make sense to me was going to be very hard! Later that day, my next door neighbor rang my doorbell several times in quick succession. When I warily opened the door, she began questioning me on my health and my mental capacity because of the lawn mower sitting in the middle of the yard. Believe it or not, the Lord guided me to tell her the story of my conversation with God, and my desire to now follow all of His promptings even when they didn't make sense. The end result was that she listened with great interest and finally accepted the Lord as her Savior after years of resisting my attempts to witness to her. Who knew that ignoring common sense could actually work miracles when directed to do so by the wise God of the Universe?

----

1. How do you feel about common sense? Is it an important component in the way you live your daily life or is it an afterthought? Explain _____
_____
_____
_____

2. Does the idea of following God completely like the characters in the Bible scare you? If so, why? _____
_____
_____
_____

3. Does the possibility of seeing great miracles happen as a result of your obedience spur you to making the hard decision of by-passing common sense if the Lord guides you to? Why or why not? _____

_____

_____

_____

4. Why do you think God asks us to do something so hard and scary as to trust His promptings when they make no sense based on our ideas of common sense behavior? _____

_____

_____

_____

5. What would it take for you to give up your dependence on common sense guidelines to show you how to act in any given situation? Would it be harder in some situations than others? If so, explain _____

_____

_____

_____

6. At the core of your being, do you believe that if God prompts you to do something that makes no sense from a human perspective, He will always come through for you ("…underneath are the everlasting arms;" Deuteronomy 33:27)? Why or why not? _____

_____

_____

_____

7. Is it possible that your desire for control over your circumstances is holding you back in your spiritual growth? If so, how do you feel about that situation? _____

_____

_____

_____

8. God gives His rewards based solely on complete obedience to His Word regardless of how hard or scary it is to follow Him instead of our own safe thought processes. Does the thought of loss of rewards help you move toward giving up control of your life? Why or why not? Just because we accomplish things that seem good and right, if they're not done according to God's will, we will get no rewards for them, and they don't count toward laying up treasure in Heaven. Is that thought a motivator to trust only the Lord instead of your own understanding? Explain

_____

_____

_____

_____

Chapter 23

SATAN'S TRICKS VERSUS GOD'S TREATS

I think we would all agree that our spiritual lives are full of treats AND tricks. God loves us so much that He's always offering us His wonderful "treats," but our enemy, the Devil, is constantly up to his old tricks. Let me ask you a few questions to see what tricks He's up to in your world:

Have you ever felt stuck in some part of your life?

Do you find yourself doing the same things over and over even though you don't like the outcome?

Do you wish you were farther along in your spiritual life, but you don't really know what's holding you back?

Do you ever secretly wonder what's wrong with you?

Do you find yourself laughing in derision under your breath when a pastor reads the verses in the Bible about having an abundant life?

Do you ever find yourself walking through life mindlessly because to really focus and to contemplate change just seems too hard and scary?

Perhaps you can relate to this word picture I'm describing:

I saw myself walking down the pathway of life only to realize it was full of large, camouflaged pits. Some of them I avoided with great ease, and some of them seemed to suck me down before I even saw they existed. Once I had fallen into one of these pits, I discovered that there was no easy way out, and I would be stuck for long periods of time before I found a way to escape. As I finally pulled my weary legs out of the pit, I realized it was so well hidden, I couldn't have been expected to see it.

As time went on, I began to be more adapt at spotting these pits, but I still fell in with a great deal of regularity. I don't know why—maybe I was careless, maybe I got distracted, maybe I forgot how badly I hated being stuck—but whatever the reason, I tried not to beat myself up when I discovered I was at the bottom of a pit again.

Eventually, I began to spot those pits with a great deal of accuracy, but for some reason, I still fell in occasionally. I realized that I now KNEW what I was doing, but hated the idea of having to change my walking patterns. When I would fall into a pit, I knew where the hidden steps were to climb out, and I would do so immediately.

Because pits always cause bumps and bruises, and because they derail me from my goals, I began to find the strength to avoid them. Now that I was determined to be pit-free, I discovered that the pits were only along the **sides** of the pathway! Some pits were just slightly off the center, and those were harder to discern. But If I purposed to keep my walking patterns straight down the center of the pathway, I missed all the pits. What a relief, and the change wasn't as hard as I thought it would be!

What pit or pits do you fall into on your particular pathway?

Perhaps it's constantly staying busy—overscheduled. Whether you're busy about the work of the Lord or just your own schedule, you feel like you must be valuable—people couldn't survive without you. Or maybe the busyness just keeps you from feeling the pain in your heart or facing the emptiness in your life.

Perhaps it's an eating or drug addiction brought on by dissatisfaction, insecurities, or disappointments. You reach for food or a pill because it tastes/feels good without even realizing, at first, that it's a craving for something better. Once you understand what that craving is, though, when you indulge, you do so rationalizing that at least food or a pill brings short-term comfort for those deep aches and longings.

Perhaps it's a relationship that you hang onto, or have unrealistic expectations for, even when to do so is destroying you. You can't imagine doing life without that relationship, or without that perspective on that relationship. You depend on it to make you feel better about yourself. You have expectations for that relationship that only God can fulfill, and so you're continually disappointed. This relationship could be a spouse, a boyfriend, a girlfriend, a family member, or even a small group.

Perhaps it's shopping. You feel like buying things gives you a jolt of excitement that is missing in your everyday life. You think if you could just decorate your house perfectly, wear the latest style clothing, dress your children so they stand out, drive the coolest car, or have the best backyard garden, you would finally find happiness. As the debt mounts, though, you keep wondering why you don't feel better. Maybe it'll take just one more trip to the store, or another session with your favorite on-line retailer and your credit card . . . .

Perhaps it's attempting to control those around you. "After all," you say, "if they would just do things my way, they would be so much happier." There's a feeling deep inside of you that calls out through fear, or hurt, or a longing to be important, leading you to believe that if you could just control your circumstances and the people around you, you would finally believe that you have value and worth. Surely then, you would find that elusive happiness.

Perhaps it's striving to be the best parent, the best employee/employer, the best spouse, the best "Christian," or the top of the class. If you could only prove to everyone that you're the best at something, perhaps you could believe it yourself.

Perhaps it's a grudge you're holding against someone. It feels right; it feels good, and gives you a sense of power over that person. Little by little, though, that grudge is starting to control your whole life, and you find yourself unable to pray effectively, unable to talk about the Lord with the same zeal you used to have, and unable to sense the presence and love of the Holy Spirit.

Perhaps it's a sexual sin that you've justified, rationalized, and covered up. "The rules don't apply to me," you've assured yourself. "God will understand my particular situation," you comfort yourself. Deep inside, though, in the middle of the night, you find yourself not so sure.

Guilt rears its ugly head, and you feel trapped between desiring the favor of the Lord and craving the enjoyment of your sin.

Perhaps it's a lying, pretending spirit. You portray yourself as someone different than who you really are. The lies come easily, almost without thinking, and you feel your secret is safe. Because people like and praise the "fake" you, you are secretly scared and insecure, fearing that someday the truth will come out. On that day you'll slip up and then all your friends will be gone.

See, the problem is that God's "treats" are free just like the candy you give out when the doorbell rings on Halloween, but we often don't know how to find the place where the free treats are being given out. That's why we need help.

Falling into pits is dangerous to your health. It causes scrapes, bruises, broken bones, and internal damage, and it requires lots of time to be spent in "recovery rooms." The alternative is health, wholeness, and walking free so that you can become the person God planned for you to be. You see, God's "treats" are that His mercies, defined as acts of kindness, compassion, or favor, are new every morning. Great is His faithfulness to us even though we're so prone to falling into pits! (*"Great is his faithfulness; his mercies begin afresh each morning."* Lamentations 3:23).

Which will it be? The same old patterns and behaviors that have caused so much pain in your life, or walking straight down the center of this glorious pathway toward the future God has waiting for you? May this year be full of God's greatest treats, and the avoidance of all of Satan's ugly tricks!

----

1. Describe what YOUR pit(s) in the pathway looks like _____

_____

_____

_____

2. On a scale of 0-10, how sick are you of falling into these pits? Why is that such an important question? _____
_____
_____
_____

3. What would it take for you to not fall into them anymore? Explain
_____
_____
_____
_____

4. What would it take for you to actually walk down only the center of the pathway? Explain _____
_____
_____
_____

5. Would you be willing to confess your sins in openness and transparency to a trusted friend? Why or why not? _____
_____
_____
_____

6. Would you be willing to join a safe accountability group? Why or why not? _____
_____
_____
_____

7. Would you be willing to see a Christian counselor as long as it took to break the hold of that particular pit in the pathway? Why or why not?
_____
_____
_____
_____

8. Do you see yourself able to walk down the center of the pathway consistently? Explain _____

_____

_____

_____

9. How would your life change if you no longer fell into pits in the pathway of your life? Give examples _____

_____

_____

_____